Preface

Kaizen is not just for the manufacturing floor. Many processes within the office environment could stand some improvement as well. In the entire lean universe, **Perfection** is always the goal. We might not be there now, but we always try, and try again. And we work continuously to perfect the process.

A company's finance, accounting, administration and support functions are not exempt from the kaizen imperative. In fact, we believe finance and accounting have a double role to play:

1. The work they do, the information they gather, the way they analyze business decisions, the data they produce ... all must support the company's lean efforts. They must continually look for ways to give operations and sales better, timelier and incontrovertible data.
2. They must do all this while making their own processes lean.

Lots of lean literature focuses on the Toyota Production System (TPS), lean manufacturing, lean accounting, continuous improvement and kaizen ... some work even focuses tangentially on the office environment. Usually, though, the office environment is only mentioned, often by stating that the standard lean methodologies can be applied in any environment, but rarely do these articles or books give you step by step instructions.

This can create difficulties for office professionals, who often haven't had training in lean concepts, the rationale and lean principles that propel continuous improvement, lean methods and tools, or participated in kaizen events. Most companies who want to tackle office kaizen quickly recognize they need education on the basics – the office kaizen "what, how, who, and why."

What: Studying an administrative or service process and improving it.
How: The improvement is done from studying the data and changing the work.
Who: The improvement is done by the people who do the work; not by outside experts.
Why: The changes are focused on providing more value for the customers.

Beyond the concepts, however, people need experience. They need to see this in action and how to apply what they see to their own company.

That's where this series of books come in.

The Cook Up Some Change series is written to help you understand what to do before, during, and after a kaizen event in the office, in a simple step-by-step format. Like a cookbook.

Good kaizen, like making good food, is something anybody can do. If you understand what you have to do and why; if your techniques are fundamentally strong; if you are using the best ingredients; and if you follow the right recipe, you will succeed.

The recipes we are laying out in this series of books will work. If you are just getting started, we strongly suggest you follow the recipes.

About the author

Dawn Wands lives in St. Louis MO, and has been working in the accounting field since 1984. She has her Master of Science, Accounting and APICS certification. Dawn has held a variety of accounting positions over her career, including Accounts Payable Mgr, Cost Accounting Mgr, Inventory Control Mgr, Lean Financial Analyst, Lean Consultant and Plant Controller. Early on she was introduced to lean and has had a passion for it ever since. She has had extensive training in both lean manufacturing and lean accounting methods.

Dawn was inspired to write this book because she is tired of accountants being stereotyped as those who resist change! In those instances where an accountant wants to improve a process, Dawn is continually asked the same question…. "Where do we start and how do we get there?"

Dawn is currently working at Aerofil Technology Inc. as a Lean Financial Analyst leading all office kaizen events as well as various other accounting responsibilities.

Contact Dawn Wands by email: dawnwands@att.net

About BMA Inc.

BMA Inc. serves the needs of companies seeking to be lean organizations, ready to meet the challenges of the 21st century. Working internationally in manufacturing, distribution, healthcare, service and financial organizations, BMA brings a team of consulting professionals that assist companies with their lean transformation. BMA consultants are experts in Lean Accounting, Lean Management Systems, and the changes required to create a truly lean organization. Our services include education, training, consulting and business counseling to companies at every stage of their lean journey to perfection.

Contact BMA Inc. by email: information@maskell.com

Cook Up Some Change:
Kaizen Recipes for the Lean Office

Book 1 in a Series

By Dawn Wands with Susan Lilly

Forward by Brian Maskell

BMA Press
Cherry Hill, New Jersey

Copyright 2012 Dawn Wands & BMA Press

BMA Inc.
100 Springdale Road
Cherry Hill NJ 08003 USA
609 239 1080
Information@maskell.com
www.maskell.com

ISBN: 978-0-9789760-2-6

Table of Contents

Preface ii
About the author iii
About BMA Inc. iii
Forward v
    Who should use this book? vi
    Lean office & accounting Diagnostic vii
    Introducing Crumple Crunch Industries (CCI) xviii
Team leaders' guide 1
    A3 – the best recipe for success 1
    Pick the best team leader 6
    Set right expectations 6
    Pick the best team 7
    Before you start 10
    Set the ground rules for the event 10
Auto-matching – improving accounts payable for raw materials: a how-to example 12
CCI's A/P kaizen event – an extended example 16
    Day 1 19
    Day 2 29
    Days 3 & 4 44
    Day 5 56
Creating a purchase order with fewer transactions: a buyers' kaizen for improving purchasing activities – another how-to example 61
    Day 1 65
    Day 2 83
    Day 3 97
    Day 4 102
    Day 5 116
What's ahead in the "Cook up Some Change" series and what's next for YOU? 120

Forward

This book has been needed for a very long time – a clear, step-by-step approach to lean kaizen improvement in the office.

Aimed at people in finance, accounting, purchasing, inventory control, production planning, HR, customer service and IT, this book will enable you to confidently move forward with radical lean improvement within your own processes and departments.

Our focus at BMA Inc. [1] is on Lean Management and Lean Accounting. While there are many important changes required to create excellent lean management and lean accounting, the starting point is to apply lean thinking in your own neck of the woods. In the accounting offices. In purchasing and the supply chain. In HR. In customer service. In shop floor planning and control and in inventory planning.

But the problem is where to start.

The book addresses the "where should I start?" question.

Human nature being what it is, we know that underlying the "where should I start?" question are the "I don't know how to do this, I don't want to mess up, I don't want to look stupid and I don't want to waste a lot of time" questions. This book addresses these issues as well.

In the Cook Up Some Change series Dawn Wands and Susan Lilly have created a cookbook of kaizen "recipes" that show how you can dish-up important lean change and improvement using the ingredients you have at your disposal.

These recipes begin by assuming that you have no knowledge of lean kaizen – you can boil water, but that's about it. The recipes show you not only what to do to eliminate waste, reduce time spent and create more value, but also they show you how to organize the events, select the team, use some common continuous improvement tools and how to ensure your success sustains over the long term.

This cookbook is not for master chefs and you don't need to have a peculiarly colored belt[2] to be successful. These recipes are for the hardworking people in the back offices of manufacturers, distributors, banks, schools, hospitals and government departments who need to get more done with their people and their time. Based firmly on lean thinking and lean principles, these practical recipes will enable you to feast on your successful improvements and have people coming back for a second plateful.

I am proud to be associated with this excellent book. And there is more to come. This book provides the basics. But over the next few months, BMA Press will be adding more books and eBooks with rich menus of recipes that will take us beyond the basics and onto satisfying platefuls for more mature lean organizations.

Brian H. Maskell,
President, BMA Inc.
Cherry Hill, NJ USA

---

[1] BMA Inc. The Lean Management Leaders +1 609 239 1080 information@maskell.com www.maskell.com
[2] With apologies to yellow belts, green belts, black belts, and the most mysterious of all - the master black belt.

Who should use this book?

This is a book for finance and accounting managers and lean leaders who are working on problems involving accounting. In his bestselling book Making the Numbers Count, Brian Maskell, President of BMA Inc.[1], spells out the rallying cry:

> "The author has observed that the attitude of accountants in companies implementing lean manufacturing varies considerably from one organization to the next. In some companies they are "on the team"—the accounting people are leaders in the quest for change and perfection. In other companies the accountants actively oppose change. The people who are bent on innovation and improvement must fight the accountants either by working around them or by the fine art of Machiavellian politicking. In most companies the accountants carry on "doing their own thing" despite the revolution taking place around their ears.
>
> If you accept the assertion that all companies must improve radically if they are to remain competitive in our "white knuckle times," then you must recognize that radical change is needed in the accounting department. The accountant must become proactive. He or she must become a leader for change and accept the change of role this requires." [2]

This book will also help you decide the most important kaizens for you to do right now using a BMA Inc. devised questionnaire or "Diagnostic" to identify gaps in the implementation of lean in your processes.

This diagnostic is designed to help you assess where you stand with regard to transitioning office processes to be lean and to support a lean organization.

We will lay out what to do using a cookbook and recipe concept. We will walk you through the kaizen, from start to finish, using detailed and realistic examples. Thus, we spell out the approach, how to lay out problem and solution in clear step-by-step format.

The maturity path concept

As you examine the Diagnostic, you will notice it's laid out in four columns titled "Traditional", "Developing a Framework," "Managing by Value Stream," and "Lean Business Management." In this book we call these "Maturity Path Levels."

New cell measurements using a lean approach are needed to track and control the new production flow. If you continue to use traditional measurements in the cells, the measurements will actively work against the success of the lean cells and pull the people back to their old ways. If you are looking for the operational improvements in the cells to be reflected in financial or bottom-line benefits, you will most likely be disappointed. Many of the benefits of lean improvement do not provide short-term financial improvement. You need another way to assess the financial impact.

It is never too early to start dismantling your company's transaction-driven control systems. They represent huge amounts of waste and cost to the organization. There are many changes that can be made at the early stages of lean, especially in response to transaction elimination. You can begin to remove a lot of the detailed reporting in the new lean cells and (perhaps) relieve inventories once the product is completed or shipped, instead of backflushing at every stage of production. Manual operations in accounts payable and receivable can be automated. By applying lean thinking to all financial accounting processes, you can eliminate a good deal of waste in the accounting office. This will

---

[1] BMA Inc., Cherry Hill NJ www.maskell.com. Email: Information@maskell.com
[2] Brian H. Maskell, *Making the Numbers Count: the accountant as change agent on the world-class team.* 2nd edition. (New York, NY: CRC Press, 2009), 4.

free-up some of the people's time to work on more important lean improvements—such as Lean Accounting for operations.

We will show you how to do this in this book and the ones to follow.

It helps to think about making improvements if you can understand your ideas in terms of a continuum. Most people who cook know the fundamentals, and as they get better at it, they understand how to take the basics to a higher level, and so on. When it comes to lean, the same is true.

We want to change the roles of finance and accounting people in our organization. We can bring more to the table for our customers if we shift the role of finance from detached evaluators of the lean results to integral members of the value stream teams.

Seems obvious, right?

But where to start? What do we do first, second, etc. and how will you know when you get where you want to go?

That's where the maturity path idea comes in.

It lets you peg your challenges and successes to an overall vision.

Lean office & accounting Diagnostic [1]

The author believes companies need a clear understanding of where they stand with reference to a maturity path that's designed to get them to their lean office goals. The questionnaire on the following pages is designed to help you do just that, with the added benefit of a broad list of kaizens you can plan to get where you want to go.

Eliminating transactions is the name of the game. By that we mean: eliminating unnecessary and wasteful transactions from a company's processes, while maintaining control of the business by putting lean controls in their place. This has to be a main focus of such efforts. It's where you can realize immediate, demonstrable improvements, both in efficiency and in cost.

You can score your own company and get an idea of where you need to begin with your improvements.

We recommend that you read the diagnostic over now; you will see as we go through this book, how to use it.

Then, when you are ready and you understand the process, come back to this section and work out where your company is now on the maturity path. Reading this book will also give you a better understanding of what's involved in getting you where you want to go.

Instructions
You will notice the assessment questionnaire below is divided into major categories and goals associated with them.

---

[1] This book uses an adaptation of the Lean Accounting Diagnostic, as developed by BMA Inc. For complete information about the Lean Accounting Diagnostic, see Brian Maskell, Bruce Baggaley, Larry Grasso, *Practical Lean Accounting. A Proven System for Measuring and Managing the Lean Enterprise*, 2nd edition. (Boca Raton, FL: CRC Press ,2012), 353.

We describe the characteristics you would expect to find in four categories from "traditional" to complete "lean business management." These represent a way to look at the maturity path.

We also list subjects for possible kaizens that can get you from one stage to the next.

Read each section thoughtfully. Also read the possible kaizens.

The idea is to a good overview of your place on the Lean Management maturity path coupled with the strength of your vision for where you want to end up. Your company will be unique, of course, but don't worry about that.

Within the assessment questionnaire, at the bottom of each section, there are three rows where you indicate how you rate your company on that topic. The scoring area looks like this:

	Traditional	Developing a Framework	Managing by Value Stream	Lean Business Management
Now (Current State)				
6 Months From Now				
18 Months From Now				

For each section, use <u>one rating per row</u>.

- Score a "2" in the "Traditional" column/ current state row, if the statements most closely describe your company now.
- Score a "2" under the column where you think that process category to be in 6 months.
- Score a "2" under the column where you think that process category to be in 18 months.

This needs a judgment call from you; done thoughtfully, this exercise gives you a good broad-brush representation about where you think your company is currently, plus when and where you see improvements happening.

Example of scoring
Here is a simple example to show how that might look. The evaluation of each of the seven process categories is as follows:

Current: This example company rated itself as "Traditional" in all seven of the categories;
Six Months for Now: "Traditional" for three of the categories and in "Developing a Framework" for the remaining four;
Eighteen Months from Now: "Developing a Framework" for four of the categories and "Value Stream Management" for the remaining three.

This example company's overall Score sheet would look as follows:

Category & Goal	Traditional	Developing a Framework	Managing by Value Stream	Lean Business Management
Now (Current State)	14			
6 Months From Now	6	8		
18 Months From Now		8	6	

Okay, now it's time for you to complete the questionnaire.

Read, think about, and score each category.

Then add up and write your own totals in the boxes below.

Your grand totals

Category & Goal	Traditional	Developing a Framework	Managing by Value Stream	Lean Business Management
Now (Current State)				
6 Months From Now				
18 Months From Now				

The assessment questionnaire

Category & Goal	Traditional	Developing a Framework	Managing by Value Stream	Lean Business Management
Accounts Payable & Procurement Shift from high volume and procedurally complex processes to minimum transactions with built in controls	Each order of materials and supplies is documented with a regular purchase order. All materials and supplies received are checked and documented. We perform a manual 3-way match to ensure the accuracy of invoices prior to entering into the system.	We have made great strides in simplifying accounts payable. We now use the system to 3-way match. We have issued blanket purchase orders for high moving material, and have started to identify and certify strategic suppliers. Systems are now in place to prepare for "pay on receipt" of materials for key suppliers.	Most of our key suppliers deliver material based on kanban. Suppliers deliver frequently (daily or twice weekly) and are set up to "pay on receipt", eliminating the need for an invoice. For slow moving or one time purchases, we use the system to 3-way match.	Materials are paid on receipt when the products are shipped. All payments are electronic and there is no AP process.
	Kaizens for Next Stage	**Kaizens for Next Stage**	**Kaizens for Next Stage**	
	Credit Cards for Small Purchases Blanket POs for Large Purchases Certify Strategic Suppliers 3-way match on computer	Eliminate three-way match Voucher for payment on receipt	Electronic payment for all suppliers Expense materials when received	
Your "Score"				
Now (Current State)				
6 Months From Now				
18 Months From Now				

Category & Goal	Traditional	Developing a Framework	Managing by Value Stream	Lean Business Management
Accounts Receivable Shift from high volume and procedurally complex processes to minimum transactions with built in controls.	We mail order acknowledgments to customers on receipt of a purchase order. We mail invoices to the customer each time we ship a product. We collect cash from late paying customers by phone calls and collection agencies.	We have greatly simplified our accounts receivable and order fulfillment processes by encouraging blanket sales orders from our key customers and by invoicing directly from shipping. Other improvements include using positive pay, on-line banking, and electronic customer account set up.	We have made steps toward eliminating the need for invoicing our key customers by encouraging them to pay us upon receipts of the materials. Increasingly we are delivering daily to customers' production lines based upon kanban orders.	We have eliminated all regular accounts receivable processes. Customers wire payments into our bank accounts for materials delivered based upon their usage of products shipped to their customers.
	Kaizens for Next Stage	**Kaizens for Next Stage**	**Kaizens for Next Stage**	
	Accept blanket sales orders from customers. Invoice directly from shipping.	Accept pay on receipt from customers. Deliver daily to customers based on kanban orders. Eliminate invoices to customers. Eliminate POs from customers for individual purchases.	Customers wire payments into our bank account. Accept payment from customers based on their usage.	
Your "Score"				
Now (Current State)				
6 Months From Now				
18 Months From Now				

Category & Goal	Traditional	Developing a Framework	Managing by Value Stream	Lean Business Management
Authorizations and Sign offs Shift from requiring signoffs and reviews to authorize transactions to building controls into the process itself	We require manual sign offs on all requisitions and purchases of expenses items. All transactions and journal entries affecting the financial statements require review and sign-off by an appropriate member of management, depending on the size of the transaction. Larger items require multiple levels of approval.	We now use procurement cards for small purchases to eliminate multiple invoices. For recurring transactions we have established arrangements with suppliers, thereby providing blanket authorization. Some recurring payments are set up to auto pay through the system.	We have pushed most of the transaction authority down to the value stream managers and have strengthened the budgetary accountability of the value stream managers. Consequently we have been able to eliminate the requirement for prior approval except on major capital expenditures.	Same as previous category.... We have pushed most of the transaction authority down to the value stream managers and have strengthened the budgetary accountability of the value stream managers. Consequently, we have been able to eliminate the requirement for prior approval except on major capital expenditures.
	Kaizens for Next Stage Eliminate multiple approvals for purchases. Push authority for purchasing down to departmental managers. Implement blanket authorization for selected items with key suppliers	**Kaizens for Next Stage** Push authority for purchasing to value stream managers. Eliminate the requirement for prior approval on all but capital expenditures.	**Kaizens for Next Stage** None.	
Your "Score"				
Now (Current State)				
6 Months From Now				
18 Months From Now				

Category & Goal	Traditional	Developing a Framework	Managing by Value Stream	Lean Business Management
Month End Shift from monthly closings of the books requiring multiple accruals and adjustments to automated closings requiring few accruals and adjustments	Preparing monthly financial package is complex and cumbersome. There are many transactions and adjustments. We often do not have the financial reports complete until 2-3 weeks into the next month.	We have greatly simplified the monthly closing process by simplifying many of the processes such as setting up reports to auto run, using the system to download information instead of manual keying. All journal entries are uploaded instead of hand keyed. Inactivated unused GL accounts. In the process we have eliminated accounts in which the costs are not material to the company as a whole. We have been able to eliminate much of our month end accruals due to the simplification of our AP, AR and inventory processes.	We are now closing the books in one working day. Most of the processes are automated due to increased operating controls implemented through lean and the greatly reduced inventory levels. We have adopted enhanced balance sheet and P&L planning through our Sales, Operations, & Financial Planning (SOFP) process. We have reliable month-end financial information ahead of the month-end.	We have automated all month-end processes, allowing preparation of financial statements without closing the books at any time during the month.
	Kaizens for Next Stage	**Kaizens for Next Stage**	**Kaizens for Next Stage**	
	Eliminate general ledger accounts and cost centers that are not material to the company as a whole. Standardize the chart of accounts across all operating units. Eliminate month end accruals related to accounts payable and receivable when kaizens in those areas have been completed.	Automate closing process. Begin the process of replacing annual budgets with 3 month rolling.	Create financial statements at any time without closing the books.	
Your "Score"				
Now (Current State)				
6 Months From Now				
18 Months From Now				

Category & Goal	Traditional	Developing a Framework	Managing by Value Stream	Lean Business Management
Material Costs Shift from multiple postings of materials to accumulate product costs to a simple accrual of value stream material costs	All production costs are tracked and controlled using a job costing system to monitor the amounts of materials used. The actual quantities of materials used are posted to a work order at each operation. We make extensive use of variance reports to monitor the actual material costs against the standard costs .	We have flattened our bills of material since more items are now moving through production without WIP. Backflusing at each stage of production is no longer necessary, thus inventory accuracy has improved.	Material costs are tracked in one of three ways. We either backflush the finished products as they are completed or shipped; this together with scrap reporting provides the material costs. Or we expense the materials to the value stream on receipt from the suppliers. Or - if the inventory level is high - we expense the materials to the value stream as they are issued to the shop floor.	We expense the costs of material directly to the value stream at the time of purchase. There is very little inventory in the plant and the cycle times are so short that materials are used as they are purchased.
	Kaizens for Next Stage	**Kaizens for Next Stage**	**Kaizens for Next Stage**	
	Create accurate and flattened bills of materials. Back flush standard material costs to relieve inventory of finished goods as they are completed or shipped.	Expense materials to the value stream as they are received from suppliers.	Expense materials to the value stream as they are purchased. (Implementation of kanban required)	
Your "Score"				
Now (Current State)				
6 Months From Now				
18 Months From Now				

Category & Goal	Traditional	Developing a Framework	Managing by Value Stream	Lean Business Management
Labor & Overhead Costs Shift from multiple postings of labor to recording labor and overhead directly to cost of sales as incurred.	All production costs are tracked and controlled using a job costing system to monitor the amounts of labor used. The actual quantities of labor used are posted to a work order at each operation. We make extensive use of variance reports to monitor the actual labor costs against the standard costs.	We have eliminated detailed labor tracking and job-step tracking. We now use labor tables that were developed using actual data based on the production schedule. The updated and improved accuracy of our bills of materials and routings allows us to automate the assignment of labor through backflushing using our standard labor costs and actual production. We have eliminated the reporting of labor and overhead variances in our costing reports.	We charge labor and overhead costs in summary directly to the value stream instead of applying them directly to production.	We charge labor and overhead costs in summary directly to the value stream instead of applying them directly to production.
	Kaizens for Next Stage	**Kaizens for Next Stage**	**Kaizens for Next Stage**	
	Eliminate detailed labor tracking and job step tracking. Improve accuracy of labor routings. Automate the assignment of labor by back flushing using standard labor costs and actual production. Eliminate detailed reporting of labor and overhead variances.	Charge labor and overhead in summary directly to the value stream instead of applying them to production. (Value Stream Costing)	None.	
Your "Score"				
Now (Current State)				
6 Months From Now				
18 Months From Now				

Category & Goal	Traditional	Developing a Framework	Managing by Value Stream	Lean Business Management
Inventory Tracking Eliminate all tracking of inventory through the production process.	We keep detailed track of our inventory--raw materials, work in process and finished goods. We enter transactions for receipts, issues, adjustments, movement between locations and miscellaneous usage of materials. Our inventory is counted through cycle counts using an ABC method. A's counted once per quarter, B's once per 6 mths, and C's once per year. Often there are many adjustments to our inventory when issues are found.	Cycle counting has become easier since we've flattened our bills of material, eliminating WIP part #'s. Since many items have a fixed location, we now count by location, and are able to count all items every month. We use the cycle counting as a way to discover the root causes of the errors created in the inventory balances in addition to maintaining the accuracy of the balances themselves. In this way we are gradually eliminating the error creating problem in our processes. Beginning stages of setting up kanbans.	We have implemented kanban-style pull control of inventory throughout the value streams. We have eliminated cycle counting for those items in a kanban because we have good visual controls of inventories in the value stream. For slower moving items (about 20%), cycle counts are still performed.	We have largely eliminated inventory tracking from our computer system due to components being expensed on receipt. A physical inventory is performed at each month end for the purpose of valuing inventory on the balance sheet. Inventory takes less than 2 hours to count due to the kanban process, making it easier to count.
	Kaizens for Next Stage	**Kaizens for Next Stage**	**Kaizens for Next Stage**	
	Improve the cycle count process to eliminate the ABC method and move to counting by locations. Use cycle counting as a way to discover root causes of errors created in inventory balances.	Implement kanban pull throughout the value stream. Implement visual control of inventory. Eliminate cycle counting. Eliminate perpetual inventory tracking of raw materials and components.	Eliminate inventory tracking from the computer system.	
Your "Score"				
Now (Current State)				
6 Months From Now				
18 Months From Now				

Interpreting the results
Take a look at your totals.

Which of these three descriptions best describes your scores?

	Beginner The majority of your scores fall into the "Traditional" and "Developing a Lean Framework" maturity path columns. You are just getting started, definitely not ready yet to cook for Buckingham Palace. You have a lot to learn from the best teachers you can find.
	Intermediate The majority of your scores fall into the "Developing a Framework" and "Lean Value Stream Management" columns. You're on your way. You are learning fast and have a much to do. But you are mastering the tools, and sometimes you even surprise yourself with your success.
	Advanced The majority of your scores fall into the "Lean Value Stream Management" and "Lean Business Management" categories. You are becoming a master chef. You know your tools, can select the best ingredients and all around you good things are happening. Others are learning from you. Buckingham Palace will be calling soon!

Next, thoughtfully re-read the "kaizens for next stage" sections.

These kaizens outline the major improvements that your company needs to move along the maturity path. Think about where your company stands now, what your priorities and resources are and where you believe you need to be. Underline the kaizen you think needs attention right now. This tells you what you might need to do first. Think about the best time frame that makes sense for your resources.

When you are done, you will have an idea of the pace at which you need get the kaizens done.

Feel free to change the wording of the kaizens if that makes them fit your company's approach. We all know variations are inevitable, just as we know all companies are different. But we also know there are great areas of similarity.

There are many ways to use this assessment tool once you have assessed the company. Here are a few examples:

- With a group of managers to focus on the need for change
- To establish a vision for your company and get buy-in from management on the direction you are going
- To achieve a priority listing of what to do first, second, etc.
- With a group of staff to transmit overall strategic direction and time frame
- ... and many more.

Introducing Crumple Crunch Industries (CCI)

CCI will be our "model" company throughout this series. You'll be seeing a lot of CCI and its people, so a brief CCI company profile is in order.

CCI was founded in 1950 when Jack Stark, a returning World War II veteran, got a job driving a bread truck. Jack's customers complained that loaves of bread that were crushed and crumpled during handling were being wasted. Jack, who had a carpentry workshop in his Brooklyn basement, set out to build the best breadboxes available and to sell these to all the local bakeries. Crumple Crunch Industries was born.

By the 1970's, CCI was making specialized packaging for many markets. If a product needed special protection from damage, CCI could build a shipping box to do the job. Expendable and returnable packaging was developed.

Today, CCI packaging is made from recycled and bio-degradable materials. Their high strength vegetable-based plastics can retain their shape and protective qualities even in extreme conditions. They lead the world in being able to protect even the most fragile products during shipment around the world.

CCI's customers include some of the planet's biggest companies. They ship all types of products, including electronics, foods and even other packaging!

Jack Stark, who now serves as Chairman Emeritus of the board, likes to say, "If you can't afford to crunch it, get Crumple Crunch to protect it." CCI is still a privately held company. It employs 450 people and is still headquartered in Brooklyn, NY.

CCI today has increasing competition from low-cost suppliers in other parts of the world. CCI is committed to implementing lean methods and plans to remain aggressively competitive in global packaging markets. CCI's management team has been schooled in lean methods.

CCI's progress has been excellent on the shop floor.

They now understand the need to bring accounting and support into the game.

CCI's management team

Steve Stark, President and Chief Executive Officer. Grandson of Jack Stark. Steve is a driving force behind becoming lean.
Anne Johnson, Chief Financial Officer.
Kathy Andersen, Controller. Kathy has the authority to authorize changes that affect accounting and control; she has direct connections with the auditors in the event auditor approvals are necessary
Jane Holmes, Accountant, Office Kaizen Leader.
John Casper, Buyer. John understands the importance of having the correct price on the purchase order, but because he is very busy it's extremely difficult to ensure perfection on his part.
Stacy Stiletto, Purchasing Manager. Stacy sets up supplier agreements and has authority to make changes that affect supplier agreements and anything else involving purchasing.

Steve Timour, another Buyer for a different value stream. Steve is fairly new to Crumple Crunch and finds his job difficult to keep up with because he's just now learning about supermarkets and also having to use MRP.
Robby Gunner, Lean Coordinator. Robby works in the lean office and has been through some extensive training setting up supermarkets and has also worked for other lean companies.
Morrie Harris, Operations Manager.

As we work through more kaizens, we'll be introducing more CCI people. And, as we proceed through this series of kaizens, we'll show you how CCI scored itself using the diagnostic, as they prepared to tackle each kaizen event.

Team leaders' guide

How do you put together the best kaizen for every situation?

A truly exhaustive treatise on how to do a kaizen (one that could cover all contingencies) would be about as huge as an unabridged English dictionary. Even printed on the thinnest paper, it would be hefty – too hefty for practical use.

Instead, what we did in this book is focus on the best recipes designed to teach basic kaizen techniques. Will they exactly match in exhaustive detail what your company is trying to do? Most likely not. Will your company have issues and problems similar to what we will address? Probably yes. Will you be able to adapt our approach to your situation? Definitely yes!

We can say this because we will be "teaching by example." All our techniques are aimed at one goal: the best possible kaizen for your company.

A great chef knows you can't skimp on ingredients, on proper, tested procedures or on the time it takes to give it your best shot. Done right, a great dish is incomparable.

The artistry involved for the chef to produce an exquisite result takes years to acquire.

Home cooks, on the other hand, have a compelling need to prepare good, nutritious food for their guests and families all the time. They rely on tested recipes, following the steps and applying the cookbook author's experience and learning. An experienced home cook with the right recipe can get a tasty dinner on the table every day, in the right quantity, to feed the family.

An excellent lean leader knows the same is true of kaizen.

A3 – the best recipe for success

For good kaizen, you need a clear understanding of where you are and where you want to be put together with a strategy for getting there.

Our Diagnostic tool gets you on the right path. Now you need a good tool to control your progress.

This is where the A3 comes in.

A3 – standard work for managing change in a company

The A3 is a problem-solving tool first used by Toyota Motor Corporation. Most A3's are handwritten. Most use simple graphics to illustrate situations, such as stick figures, storm clouds, numbers, circles, arrows, etc.

If you are just starting, it's important to use the A3 method chosen for our recipes. Of course you can tailor the A3 to suit your company as you gain experience. But do use an A3!

In the best lean companies, using the A3 is standard work. It's your best tool to document why an event was chosen (the issues), the target condition, and the confirmed state once your changes are in place. You will use the A3 throughout your kaizen events to keep the team focused on the right stuff. The A3 is our best recipe for success.

In her article for Lean Directions: the on line magazine for lean manufacturing, C. Jimmerson succinctly lays out the reasons for using the A3.

Here's a summary of Jimmerson's list:

> The A3 is objective. It uses diagrams and simple graphics to create understanding. Hand drawn is best.
> The A3 helps understand root causes
> The A3 makes creating the target condition easy
> The A3 clearly lays out accountability
> The A3 establishes the basis for testing alternatives.
> With the A3 everyone learns to see problems the same way
> A3 problem solving occurs as part of everyday work
> A3 problem solving is intuitive and easy to learn and remember
> A3 thinking means better and fewer meetings
> The A3 process documents costs and benefits
> The A3 template helps us solve problems and document new processes
> The A3 process is satisfying to everyone, particularly frontline workers;
> The A3 is easy to learn and easy to teach. [1]

Get your team up to speed on how to use an A3

If your team is not experienced with kaizen, you will need to do some training on how to use this essential tool. We will be dealing with training as a separate issue in this series, but for now, we'll stick with the essentials of the A3.

Something like this needs to be part of your team's training. You can do this with a study group, a class ... whatever works best for your company.

---

[1] Jimmerson, C. "*A3 Problem Solving: Simplicity At Work,*" Society of Manufacturing Engineers http://www.sme.org/cgi-bin/get-newsletter.pl?LEAN&20060309&2& (accessed October 2011)

Here's our layout for an A3. We created this with a computer to make it easy to see the individual A3 components. Usually, you would do this by hand on a large piece of paper. This is the A3 template we will use throughout this book to demonstrate our examples.

Event Title: List Event Title here Team Leader: List Team Leader name & title here Co-Leader: List Co-leader name & title here Consultant: List Consultant name here	Team: List Team Members & Titles here	Event Date: List event dates here Today's Date: List todays date here
Reason Event was Chosen <u>complete this portion before event</u>	**Current State** <u>complete this portion During event</u>	**Rapid Experiments** <u>complete this portion During event</u>
Initial State <u>complete this portion before event</u>	**Ideal State** <u>complete this portion During event</u>	**Confirmed State** <u>complete this portion During event</u>
Target Conditions <u>complete this portion before event</u>	**Benefit/Effort Matrix** <u>complete this portion During event</u>	**Completion Plan** <u>complete this portion During event</u>

Figure 1 Components of Our A3

Let's go through this A3 piece by piece.

Descriptive material at the top of the A3

Title:

A Brief Description of the Event: Be sure to include what you want to accomplish when the event is over. For example, do not type "Accounts Payable" or "Expense Report". Use verbs.

If your goal is to reduce the time it takes to process an invoice and also remove waste from the process, you can describe the event something like "Remove Waste from Processing an Invoice".

The A3 is the main document describing your event. Many times this is the document the company's management will review before approving an event. Be clear! Here's an example: "Eliminate manual matching in A/P." See, there's a verb!

Members of the team:

Team Leader: List the name and title of the team leader.

The team leader needs to design the A3 so it depicts a clear vision of the goals and objectives of the event. It's the job of the leader to keep the team focusing on the goals of the A3, while challenging the team as outlined in this manual.

Co-Leader: List the name and title of the co-leader (if you have one.) Co-Leaders are future leaders in training. Sometimes they also serve as the assistant to the Team Leader for larger groups.

Team Members: List the names and titles of all the team members.

Facilitator: List the name and title of the facilitator (if you have one.)

In some companies there are people specifically working on process improvement. Sometimes these are called "The Lean Resource Team", "Process Improvement Team", or "Kaizen Promotion Office", just to name a few. These people act as facilitators to help train the team, schedule events, provide kaizen materials, coordinate presentations and facilitate events.

Consultant: List the name of the outside consultant and the name of the company if you are using one.

Many companies hire consultants to facilitate kaizen events. This is especially helpful in the beginning stages of kaizen, and possibly long-term for companies that don't have the resources to invest in a "Process Improvement Team" on site. The consultant's role varies depending on the time available and the capabilities and experience of the company employees.

Event dates: Dates of the event.

Information in the body of the A3

Reason improvement was chosen:

A list all of the current issues that show why you are doing the kaizen event. Many times the problems are the direct opposite of the target conditions.

Write problem statements and situations so these are CLEAR to the team and to management. The problem statement should indicate the scope of the kaizen as well.

Remember: No problem = No justification for a kaizen event. If you can't make this clear, then there's no reason to do the kaizen!

Get this section done before you begin the event.

Initial state:

Process information always helps the team get familiar with the situation before beginning the event. If you have process maps that demonstrate the initial state, so much the better!

In our recipes, we list the essential facts about the current process, including: the approximate time to process an invoice in accounts payable; other issues, etc. Be sure to add your information (even if estimated) about the volumes involved: How many people? How many invoices? How much time each invoice takes, etc.

It is important to include real data about the process. Making this information as specific as possible helps quantify the task and also helps you measure the proposed solution.

Target conditions (often called the "future state")

Describe what it is you're trying to accomplish. Quantify each target if there are several target conditions for one event. For example, "automate 3-way match", or "reduce lost discounts by 50%".

Targets are based on estimates. Set your goal high, but be realistic. As your teams get more experienced, and if they have the best and most "real" information going in, they will get better at estimating and setting goals.

CAUTION: Don't let the team "low ball" the goals to make the results look better. You should critically examine whether your goal could be more ambitious. Your team should be ready to stretch.

When deciding on targets, consider the length of the event and the level of knowledge of each team member. Too many targets will cloud the event, resulting in reduced success. Having people involved who have little relevant knowledge can make an event difficult.

Look again at Figure 1 above. The underlined information shows the timing for completing each A3 section.

You should complete the first three boxes on the A3 before the kaizen event begins. This will require some preliminary work from yourself and/or the team, and often collection of data, so build this into your schedule.

Fill in the rest of the boxes as the event progresses.

Pick the best team leader

For best results, choose a team leader with a strong resume. The best team leader for your kaizen will have these attributes:

- Possesses a deep understanding of the company's strategic goals and objectives
- Is passionate about removing waste
- Can motivate team members to think creatively
- Is currently a leader in the company or has the proven ability to lead a team
- Is a good coach and can facilitate the team with an open mind
- Can take control and make final decisions if necessary
- Wants to develop future team leaders
- Will never accept an answer like: "We've already tried that and it doesn't work," or "That's impossible."

Set right expectations

Make sure the team leader and everybody on the team understand the expected results. A kaizen event may positively benefit many areas, specifically in the areas shown at right.

> - Standardizing processes, i.e., creating new standard work
> - Eliminating lots of waste (non-value added transactions)
> - As a training tool
> - Saving time and creating business opportunities by creating available capacity
> - Eliminating the opportunity for error by perfecting the process

IMPORTANT NOTE (before you try this at home)

Everyone on the kaizen team needs to know that no full-time employees will be laid off as a result of improvements.

People won't cooperate willingly if they believe they are working themselves out of a job.

As kaizen produces improvements, for example, as cycle time decreases, this means specific tasks will take less time than before. It will become clear to the team that specific areas may warrant some re-arranging. So your team must be ready to brainstorm alternatives.

Alternatives to laying off full time people should include:

- Eliminating any temporary employees
- Not hiring new employees in cases where new business is expected
- Not hiring new employees as attrition happens

- Cross training to balance the work load
- Reassigning people to different areas
- Assigning people to more continuous improvement projects
- Eliminating or reducing overtime

These decisions may not be under the team leader's control. Everyone should be aware that the long-term effects of improvement activities make will bring these issues to the surface, especially as your team reports the improvements to management. Of course, the company's goal is always to do more with less.

The kaizen team needs to understand these realities and that what happens after kaizen may be out of their hands.

Pick the right kaizen to begin

At this point, people usually ask "What area do I tackle first"? Your work with the Diagnostic tool will guide you on this.

Don't waste a lot of time deciding what to do, at least not in the beginning stages of kaizen. By the time you devise a strategy for what to do, you could finish many kaizens. Kaizen, like cooking, is largely learned by doing.

As a rule of thumb, it's best to start with a small process. Some examples are:

- Processing an expense report
- Balancing a bank statement
- Balancing and distributing petty cash
- Doing a repetitive piece of the monthly financial close
- Processing an invoice for payment

The purpose for starting with a small process is to get comfortable with the kaizen process. Experience will help people understand about kaizen and the team will get stronger, as they work at it.

Think about it and ask this question: What would you rather have: kaizen that is perfect out of the box, or kaizen that moves you toward your goals and teaches you what you need to learn?

After the team has finished a few kaizen events, company management will be more familiar with the process and the benefits; then you can begin prioritizing events based on the broader goals and objectives of the organization. As people begin to see benefits and understand the process, they usually have no problem suggesting future events. Employees will often request events on their own.

As for prioritizing kaizen events, that's where the Diagnostic tool can really help.

Pick the best team

One of the most important cooking tasks is to **assemble the very best ingredients** you can find for the recipe: really fresh, the best for the task and in the right amounts.

A great chef knows this is stacking the deck in favor of success.

This is doubly true when planning kaizen events. In kaizen, the object is to effect change. The best people, with the right training, the right mindset and in the right number to do this belong on the team.

Who should always be included?

- The team leader (usually a manager or trained lean leader.)
- The person or people who do the actual work. For example, if you are working on improving the process of balancing the bank statement, you would have the person who currently does this job on the team. Given the right encouragement, this person is often the one who knows best how to improve the process.
- A backup person (if available.)
- Anyone else who has input to the process.
- Anyone, even outside the group, who can bring fresh eyes. This helps generate new ideas.
- At least one IT person, especially if you're working with computer systems and system capabilities.
- A decision maker/manager, if the manager is not already of the team. This is important so decisions can be approved as these come to the surface.

Usually, a group of five to seven works best. With four or fewer people, there may not be enough to generate new ideas. With 10 or more, the group becomes unwieldy.

Give team members ample notice that their attendance is <u>required</u> for the event. Usually two weeks' notice is enough time.

Plan enough time for the kaizen event itself

An event can last anywhere from 3 to 5 days.

Make sure you allow enough time for your kaizen event.

Often, after the event is complete, there is a "to-do list" that includes additional improvements that were not completed during the kaizen event. Sometimes these improvements are upstream or downstream of your process and may require a kaizen event in another area.

If your "to-do list" is more than one page, your kaizen event probably should have been longer or your scope narrower.

> **Remember:**
>
> A good kaizen event includes implementing the changes, not just designing them.
>
> What chef would assemble all the best ingredients for the soufflé, break the eggs, mix everything up just right, then not put it in the oven to bake?

Only if <u>absolutely unavoidable</u> should you block out time periods spread across several weeks for a kaizen event.

Here's why we don't recommend this: It is important to keep momentum and enthusiasm up, and to see demonstrable results. It's a reality, some team members cannot be away from their daily job for a long period of time, so take this into consideration when choosing the team and setting up the scope and duration of your kaizen event.

Lunch and snacks are always a plus.

Plan the sequence of the kaizen event

An outstanding cook uses recipes that lay out the best sequence to ensure excellent results. Having farm- fresh eggs and butter will not help make a great cake, if no one knows what to do first, second, third etc. The same is true for kaizen.

Having the best ingredients—leadership, dedicated team members, good time-management and a well-chosen goal – won't be enough if you go at the process in the wrong order.

Here is our recommendation for the best sequence for an event.

Sometimes, with experience, you might have to deviate from these steps. That's okay, if required. Sometimes you might want to eliminate some steps entirely. But taking short cuts without understanding the reasons for the process can get you into trouble.

So we recommend that if you are just starting out, that you follow the procedure closely.

Don't worry. As you get more experience conducting events, you will get a better at handling variable situations quickly and efficiently, as they arise.

Kaizen Steps (Procedure)	
Day 1	a. Document the current state. This lays out what you do now. b. Walk through the current process to observe and verify that you have captured the current state correctly. We call this Gemba, and it's no place for taking short cuts.
Day 2	a. Lay out the Ideal state – this is ideally where you want to end up. b. Brainstorm ideas for how you will move from the current state to the ideal state. c. Rate your ideas using a benefit vs. effort matrix. d. Prepare for rapid experiments (may involve setting meeting times with other departments) and gathering information.
Days 3 and 4	a. Do some rapid experiments to get a feeling for what the team can accomplish during and after the kaizen. b. Do a test or simulation to see that the process works. Use time and effort observations to verify results. People will feel free to make adjustments and apply the best ideas to the problem if you've got the best team with permission to be creative and experiment freely. c. Review whether it's possible to get to the ideal state within 90 days. If not, create a confirmed state which is somewhere between current & ideal state. d. Create a completion plan and assign individual responsibilities for achieving the actions. e. Prepare your team's report.
Day 5	a. Report to management and get the green light. b. Implement the changes

Figure 2 Our Recommended Sequence for Successful Kaizen

Supplies you will need for the kaizen

The chef needs a well-equipped kitchen in order to be efficient. She doesn't want to go searching for mixing tools or measuring cups in the middle of making something happen. Similarly, you need to make sure your team has what it needs, rounded up and ready to go in the event room. Here's a list:

An easel and easel pads. Ones with "stickie" sheets are nice, because you can tear them off the pages and post them on the walls easily. Square-ruled sheets are handy.

Masking tape.

Lots of Post-it® notes in a variety of colors

- 4-8 Black fine point markers. We don't recommend extra fine-point markers. Team members seated in the room won't be able to read the chart easily.
- 1 red marker
- 1 blue marker
- 1 green marker
- Pens/pencils
- Note pads for team members
- A stop watch (for measuring observations)
- A calculator
- Clip boards

Before you start

So you can make efficient use of the team's time, you may need to help people back-fill their knowledge of lean. This is probably going to be needed at the outset for office kaizens, because it's usually the case that people in the office have not been involved in making operations improvements.

If this involves reading and discussion groups, classes, or other such activities, be sure to build this into the planning.

Orient your team

Here are some of the activities you can arrange for your team as necessary:
- Formal lean training (on-site, off-site or web-based)
- Reading materials, including books and articles
- Reading discussion groups (facilitated by a lean leader)
- Training on standard problem solving methods (For example, make a book such as <u>Memory Jogger 2</u> [1] available to the team.

Conduct interviews, do observations, gather data about the subject

The team leader should make some observations of the subject. Be sure the people involved know why you are watching them. This will give you valuable background data and make it easier for you to lead the discussions during the kaizen.

Set the ground rules for the event

Okay, now you're ready to start cooking!

---

[1] M. Brassard, D. Ritter, *The Memory Jogger 2 Tools for Continuous Improvement and Effective Planning,* Second Edition (GOAL/QPC, 2010)

You've completed the first three steps of the A3 document so you have a clear vision of the goals and objectives of the event. You've picked the best team, decided on goals, trained up you team, gathered preliminary data, secured management support. It's time to gather the team and get them started off on the right foot.

1ˢᵗ Meeting

During the first team meeting, cover the following topics:

Introductions: make sure everyone knows everyone else and understands everyone's role in the company.

The A3: use A3 and re-cap the goals and objectives of the event and the benefits of accomplishing those goals. Make sure everyone knows what is going to happen.

Team Conduct: set the behavior and conduct guidelines for the team members. At minimum, include these:

- Be on time! This is essential, so team members can make the best possible use of the time set aside for the kaizen. It also demonstrates respect for the process and an understanding of the seriousness management attaches to it.
- Set specified times and location for breaks and lunch.
- Let the team know the rules for the discussion.
- Let the team know if meals and/or snacks will be provided.
- No laptops unless the group is asked to gather information that necessitates a laptop.
- No cell phones.
- If you have visitors present for the kaizen, let them know the essentials about the location.

You should include any other important or location-specific guidelines or policies as necessary, for example where they can get messages at break times; sign-in, sign-out procedures, etc.

Auto-matching – improving accounts payable for raw materials:
a how-to example

CCI will be our "model" company throughout this series.

CCI has increasing competition from low-cost suppliers in other parts of the world. CCI is committed to implementing lean methods, and plans to remain aggressively competitive in global packaging markets. CCI's management team has been schooled in lean methods.

Their progress has been excellent on the shop floor.

They now understand the need to bring accounting and support into the game.

CCI wants to improve their accounts payable process

So here we are in the 21st century. Most companies are using a computer to perform 3-way match, right? Not so fast!

The truth is that many companies have capabilities included within their computerized systems to do 3-way matching. But this doesn't always help unless their internal processes are working properly. They wind up doing manual paper matching anyway and wasting many hours of non-value added time.

When you get right down to it, whether computerized or manual, matching up virtual or physical pieces of paper after receiving a shipment from your supplier is pure waste.

This is exactly what is happening at Crumple Crunch Industries (CCI)

Does the scenario in Figure 3 look familiar?

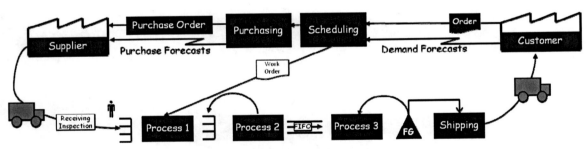

Figure 3 CCI is Making Operational Improvements

CCI has made improvements in operations, making inventory flow smoothly between processes on the shop floor. MRP / ERP does the scheduling. They have set up a few select supermarkets and have reduced the number of people it takes to keep raw materials supplied to production.

Purchasing, working with the buyers, generates, sources and places the PO's. The suppliers then ship the raw materials, it's received, inspected and placed in the supermarket. Receiving people gather together the paperwork for Accounting.

Production commences, withdrawing materials, and Accounting matches the paperwork, reviews for discrepancies, and pays the supplier if there are no problems.

Chances are your company fits somewhere into this scenario. Just a cursory look at the activities that ensue from scheduling an order shows many opportunities for improvement. To put it bluntly, there are also many opportunities for mistakes. So many in fact, sometimes companies don't know where to start.

CCI has invested in an expensive computerized system for keeping track of all aspects of their process.

Recipe for change

The truth is, there is no magical recipe that will fit all types of companies, systems, or people.

The Cook Up Some Change series can get you going.

Understand the basic process, and Voila! You know "how to boil water."

But real companies have real issues to tackle, just as a chef eventually needs to know how to serve real food, not just hot water!

We will show you how Crumple Crunch Industries (CCI) began, by walking you through their kaizen to implement improvements in their Accounts Payable operations.

CCI wants to start using the automated 3-way match that is included in their computerized system.

Management assigned accountant Jane Holmes, their Office Kaizen Leader, to the case.

The team leader studies the problem at CCI

Jane began by thinking about the problem.

When a company is still manually matching a paper invoice to a paper purchase order and a paper packing slip, there will be many reasons why they don't want to rely on a computer to do this job. These might include:

    People don't trust the system

    People don't know how to set up the system to do matching

    People don't have time to set up the system to do matching

    The system is set up to do matching, but a lot of issues come up so it's easier to resolve the issues before inputting into the system. This creates double waste, because people chase down the problems, fix them on paper, then input them into the system just so the system can match them! Reasons for this include things like:

      1. The purchase orders frequently do not match the invoice price causing manual approvals.
      2. There are many additional charges for freight, surcharges, plate charges, etc, and people are not sure how to set up the system to handle those extra charges.
      3. Quantities received or part numbers frequently do not match what was ordered, causing manual work.
      4. People feel more comfortable seeing and touching the documents, or they've always been doing it a certain way and do not want to change.

Many times accounting people feel it's their responsibility to fix all the issues caused by other departments. They think of themselves as a "back stop." As a result, other departments grow to depend on accounting to catch their mistakes. Other departments don't feel the need to make sure errors don't happen in the first place.

CCI applies the Diagnostic

Category & Goal	Traditional	Developing a Framework	Managing by Value Stream	Lean Business Management
Accounts Payable & Procurement Shift from high volume and procedurally complex processes to minimum transactions with built in controls	Each order of materials and supplies is documented with a regular purchase order. All materials and supplies received are checked and documented. We perform a manual 3-way match to ensure the accuracy of invoices prior to entering into the system.	We have made great strides in simplifying accounts payable. We now use the system to 3-way match. We have issued blanket purchase orders for high moving material, and have started to identify and certify strategic suppliers. Systems are now in place to prepare for "pay on receipt" of materials for key suppliers.	Most of our key suppliers deliver material based on kanban. Suppliers deliver frequently (daily or twice weekly) and are set up to "pay on receipt", eliminating the need for an invoice. For slow moving or one time purchases, we use the system to 3-way match.	Materials are paid on receipt when the products are shipped. All payments are electronic and there is no AP process.
	Kaizens for Next Stage	Kaizens for Next Stage	Kaizens for Next Stage	
	Credit Cards for Small Purchases Blanket POs for Large Purchases Certify Strategic Suppliers 3-way match on computer	Eliminate three-way match Voucher for payment on receipt	Electronic payment for all suppliers Expense materials when received	
Your "Score"				
Now (Current State)	2			
6 Months From Now		2		
18 Months From Now				

Figure 4 How Jane Used the Diagnostic to Get Her Bearings

CCI defines the scope of the kaizen event

Jane understood that doing 3-way matching on the computer will not move immediately into total "Lean Business Management." But she also recognized it's a necessary step along the way, and a good place to get started.

Jane spent a day observing the current process and interviewing the people involved.

One of the first things Jane learned was that John Casper (the buyer) knows that Kim (the A/P clerk) is going to show up at his desk every Monday morning with a folder an inch thick containing invoices where the price on the invoice doesn't match the price on the PO.

John has to approve these invoices. Kim is very friendly and enjoys talking with John as he signs the invoices. Even though John knows some suppliers have tiered pricing, he can't be bothered to look up the price each time so he lets the system default to the last price paid for that item.

What is happening here?

Well, it's obvious Kim is enabling John to continue with this careless behavior. Rather than asking John to verify the prices before a problem occurs, Kim is making sure she catches them downstream. John gets to remain careless; Kim gets to be a hero.

Does this sound familiar? Or maybe you're thinking this type of scenario doesn't happen at your company. Think again! This or other situations like this happen more than we (as managers) may want to believe.

Kaizen, which will get at the root causes of this situation, will fix the broken process and allow both John and Kim to do their work more effectively.

In this author's experience, many accounting people enjoy "helping" other departments when what they are really doing is supporting the wrong behavior. These people feel a sense of accomplishment for getting to be a "hero" and catching and fixing problems. Or sometimes it's job security.

The issue is that babysitting (which we like to call it), does not allow accountants to focus on the important stuff, or the issues that could potentially cost the company substantial sums of money.

During her meeting with Kim, Jane discovered that Kim spent 25% of her time processing expense reports, leaving less time to focus on raw material processing. Lack of attention to raw materials processing had become de facto "accepted practice."

Jane already knew about one serious mistake that dramatically illustrated the problem. One Friday right before a holiday, the Receiving department made a huge mistake which neither Kim nor John caught. A unit of measure of thousands on a PO was mistakenly received as 1000 instead of a single unit. This caused the invoice to be overpaid by $1,000 for each unit. This particular invoice was overpaid by $100,000! Believe it or not, the check for over $100,000 made its way to the supplier. Luckily for Crumple Crunch, the supplier was trustworthy and returned the check.

So, while this sort of error slipped through the cracks, Kim would review each expense report so closely that she would find small errors amounting to nickels and dimes each week. Of course, she was congratulated by her manager, and was proud to catch other people's mistakes. We're not saying that Kim should not be careful and thorough, but from CCI's point of view, was Kim spending her time where she could do the most good?

Most people would agree Kim's time would be better spent on the raw material end, which also happens to be 80% of Crumple Crunch's expenses.

Jane concluded Kim was too focused on expense reports; she did not give enough attention to what was really important.

But before going down the hall to call Kim on the carpet, Jane needed to ask:

   Is there Standard Work or a well documented procedure in place for the A/P Clerk position?

> If yes, is it being followed?
>
> If no, the process is broken.
>
> Does the A/P Clerk know that raw materials are the single most important part of her job? Odds are the answer is "no".
>
> Is the workload too heavy? We'll go out on a limb here, but we doubt Kim's manager really knows at this point.

Generally speaking, most employees come to work and want to feel a sense of accomplishment. Could that be the reason Kim is enabling John??? Mmmmm? It's quite possible. She may not feel that other parts of her job give her that sense of accomplishment.

That's where we come in. Let's help Kim and all other A/P Clerks around the world feel that sense of accomplishment with the work they do when they do it right.

It's very important that we change Kim's job, as we are about to do, so she still feels important and invested in the change. The $100,000 mistake might have been avoided had there been a robust back stop (the computerized 3-way match) behind both John and Kim.

Crumple Crunch decided to do a kaizen event to put the necessary changes into place.

Here's what CCI did. It's a good example of how to conduct kaizen.

CCI's A/P kaizen event – an extended example

Jane picks a team

We can't stress enough how critical it is to have great team composition for any kaizen event. But for a kaizen event focused on a process where very few people (sometimes only 1) do that job, you may well encounter some type of resistance. In many smaller companies, A/P fits that description. In those instances, it is imperative someone in an accounting management role is included in the event.

For accounts payable, as you pick a kaizen team, think about the areas that impact or are affected by A/P.

Some of our suggestions for team members:

> A/P Clerk – Person who does the work.
>
> Receiving Clerk or Manager – Person who receives and inspects raw materials. Receiving is upstream from A/P, and they record what is received, units of measure, etc.
>
> Buyer – Person who places raw materials orders. Buyers are upstream from Receiving, and impact purchase price & quantity.
>
> Accounting Manager – The person to help make decisions, when a higher level decision maker is needed.
>
> IT person – In this event an IT person can help with understanding software capabilities and limitations.
>
> Outsiders – Anyone with an open mind, willingness to change and offer new ideas. Previous kaizen training would be helpful or if this person has familiarity with the software system.

We think it's important to note that in a larger company at least 1/2 to 1/3 of the A/P Clerks should be present. And yes, physically present. No virtual or on-line meetings. Face to face contact works best. Plus, it's amazing how one kaizen event develops relationships. After the event, those A/P people who attended will communicate with each other about issues and opportunities on their own. There will definitely be less competition and more team work going forward. How wonderful is that!

Besides herself Jane chose the following people to be on the kaizen team:

>Kim Stanley – A/P Clerk
>
>Sandy Conley – Receiving Clerk
>
>John Casper – Buyer
>
>Kathy Anderson – Controller
>
>Joe Johnson – IT Support

Jane sets up the A3

Everyone on the team needs to be clear: the target condition for this event is to be able to auto-match accounts payable.

Figure 5 shows the start of the A3 based on Jane's research.

Event Desc	Eliminate manual matching in A/P				
Team Leader: Jane Holmes		Co-Leader:	Consultant:		
Event Date: 3/14/11-3/18/11		Today's Date: 3/4/2011	Team:	Kathy Andersen(Controller) Kim (A/P Clerk) Sandy (Receiving Clerk) Joe (IT Support) John Casper (Buyer)	

		Audit #	Auditor Name	Target Date	Date Complete
1. Reason Event was Chosen Eliminate Manual matching in A/P and move to auto-match using current software Remove waste and non-value-added steps Write standard work for new process		30 Day Audit		4/3/2011	
		60 Day Audit		5/3/2011	
2. Initial State No formal standard work 3-Way manual paper match (PO, Pkg slip, Invoice) About 3 minutes to process each invoice Invoice price sometime mismatches (approx. 15%) Invoice quantity sometimes mismatches (approx. 5%)		90 Day Audit		6/2/2011	
3. Target Conditions Automate the 3-way match Remove waste and non-value-added work Write standard work for new process					

Figure 5 CCI's A3 Defines the Observed Problem

Observations recorded on the A3

1. Reason Event was Chosen

   Eliminate Manual matching in A/P and move to auto-match using current software

   Remove waste and non-value-added steps

   Write standard work for new process

2. Initial State

   No formal standard work

   3-Way manual paper match (PO, packing slip, invoice)

   About 3 minutes to process each invoice

   Invoice price sometime mismatches (approx. 15%)

   Invoice quantity sometimes mismatches (approx 5%)

3. Target Conditions

   Automate the 3-way match

   Remove ALL waste and non-value-added work.

 Day 1

We have essentially 5 days to complete the kaizen and lay everything out on the A3.

On Day 1 we have the following tasks to complete:

Assemble the team – the preliminaries

The team leader gets started with introductions.

Ask each team members in turn to introduce himself. Ask each person to give the others information about his role within CCI.

> In larger companies, it's not uncommon to find that some team members do not know everybody on the team. This is especially true of office kaizens.

Only if everyone already knows everyone else, should you dispense with this step, or use an "ice breaker" exercise. The team leader can make this determination.

Once introductions are complete, the team leader gives a brief description and lays out the scope of the event based on the A3 described earlier. Give each team member a copy of the A3. Post one in the room.

On a clear wall, line up the sticky easel pads side by side. Start with two or three. Add more if needed.

Ask someone in the group to be the scribe.

Document the current state

If you are a small company like CCI with one A/P clerk, you're obviously documenting a process performed by only one person.

If, on the other hand, you are a larger company with many A/P clerks, it is VERY important each of the A/P clerk's processes is documented separately.

It's too easy for different A/P clerks to just "agree" they perform the same steps, but if you document each one separately, you will most likely see substantial differences. This is important, because we are working to improve the entire process and to create new standard work for all.

Begin with the A/P clerk that is the least knowledgeable or has the most manual process. If you start with a "super star", it may be hard for the others to follow, thinking expectations are unrealistic or too high.

Work as a group with the person who does the raw materials accounts payable. At CCI, Kim was the A/P person.

The team's task is to identify each step of the process.

Write each step on a separate Post-it®.

Figure 6 Using Post-it® Notes to Build a Chart

Do not use the computer to generate the process chart. Neatness is not important at this point. Kaizen events are not a competition for artistic talent.

Post-it® notes are best, because they are easy to re-arrange as necessary. Getting a complete understanding of the process is all that's important at this point.

We are using computer-generated illustrations because these are easily reproducible in a book. But, during a live kaizen, Post-it® notes, sketches, stick figures, etc., are just fine.

Laying out all the process steps will make the waste (non value-added activity) obvious.

We don't know your system or what types of issues are preventing your company from turning the key to auto-matching, but we've participated in quite a few similar events, and there are usually issues like those listed below.

Typically what we see are:

Person opening the mail doesn't know how to sort if properly

PO price doesn't match the Invoice price

PO quantity doesn't match the invoice quantity

Item # received doesn't match item # on the invoice

Unit of measure on the invoice is different than stocking unit of measure

PO # isn't on the invoice

Additional charges appear unexpectedly on the invoice, for example fuel surcharges, plates, dies, pallet charges, wait fees, etc.

The invoice is received in advance of the receipt in the system. Thus, there is nothing to match.

Remember, there may be steps in the process that can be eliminated even if they are not considered waste. For example, invoices are usually received by US mail. Perhaps they can be e-mailed instead (eliminating waste in the mail room.) Or if a report is routinely printed, ask "who uses it?" Maybe no one! It can be eliminated.

Just stick with the process until you have everything captured.

You may end up with a very detailed current state. This is good! It means you are finding more opportunities to eliminate waste and non-value added activities.

Important Note: Figure 7 below is an extremely simplified version of an A/P process.

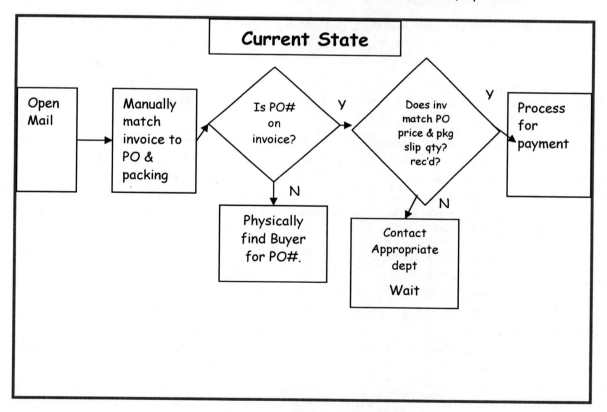

Figure 7 - CCI's Current State Process Chart

The diamond shaped Post-it® notes (a Post-it® turned at an angle) represent questions. The rectangular ones represent steps in the process.

Usually, but not always, questions point to possible "waste" or "non-value" added steps in the process. Let's go through how our CCI's team developed this diagram.

Kim, the A/P clerk, began by narrating how she handles an invoice from the beginning to end of the process. Her 1st step is to "open the mail." This was then hand written on a Post-it® and placed on the chart.

Team Leader Jane then asked questions about the process, intended to clarify how the process actually works with as much specificity as possible, such as:

> How many invoices do you receive in a day?
>
> Do you pick up the mail from a lock box or is it delivered to you?
>
> When does the mail get delivered?
>
> Do you open all the mail or just invoices?
>
> How long does it take you to open the mail?
>
> How long does it take you to process all the invoices you get?

> **Remember, at this point you are only asking questions.**
>
> **Do not try to develop solutions just yet.**

We can't stress strongly enough: do this at the gemba! This is not intended to be only a "table top" exercise, and there's no substitute for actually going to where the work is being done and watching what's happening. In any case, the results of the discussion should always be verified by observation.

These types of questions are important because they pin down actual data when dealing with continuous improvement. The team's analysis needs to be based on data, not just hunches or guess work.

The team will eventually want to demonstrate with facts how the process will improve. It's important to know how many invoices are received because down the road the team will think about "auto pay" or "pay on receipt" options. Both are automated ways of processing payment without an invoice. It's really important to develop as much and as accurate information about a process at this point. When you do arrive at the point where you brainstorm solutions, you can be certain the team has what it needs to seek and find good solutions.

If other team members begin offering suggestions for improvement, kindly let them know that there will be plenty of time for that later. Explain again, if necessary, this stage of the event is meant to "document reality". It works best and gets realistic, honest contributions from everybody, if the team is focused only on describing the process.

> **Note to Team Leaders:** as you prepare for the event, you might find a particular member of the team that people see as "difficult." If you foresee this on your team, it's best to have that person's manager present.

The Team Leader should challenge the team to disclose as much as possible relevant information. Asking questions is a good way to do this. Questions like: "Why wouldn't the mail be clearly identified?" or "Why do you have to find a person to approve the invoice?" are examples how you can begin to identify waste in the process.

As the team digs deeper into the process of documenting reality, the Team Leader needs to ask, "Approximately how long do you have to wait between steps in the process?" Understanding wait time is critical because the amount of waiting influences how the process does or doesn't flow. Even small wait times are important. Over a day or a week, they will add up to significant time wasted. Moreover, waiting that gets to be a habit, inhibits flow and creates opportunity for errors.

Questions that start with the word "why" stimulate the brains of the team members. Asking "why" many times will usually lead to the root cause of most problems.

Team members are not always willing to share information. In some instances, employees will hold back information for fear of losing their job. The Team Leader should remind people that the current process isn't "wrong." It has worked from the time it was developed. In this case Jane said "We are about making improvements. If we want to make what we do better, we have to start with understanding how and why we are doing it."

Despite the Team Leader's best efforts, some people will refuse to participate meaningfully. In those instances, continue asking questions until you get the information required. As you become experienced as a Team Leader, you can usually tell when a person is holding back information about the process.

If the person is explaining a process and it appears there is no waste in the process, you may consider asking special questions to get at this.

For example, using the current state in our example, suppose Kim initially neglected to say what happens when the paperwork doesn't match up. The Team Leader needs to ask, "Is PO number always on the invoice?" and "Does the invoice always match PO & the packing slip?" "What happens when the paperwork does not match?" The Team Leader may not be familiar enough with the details of the process to know if steps or decisions were omitted. But you can safely assume the process is not error free, or you wouldn't be trying to make improvements.

In our example, Jane kept probing.

"Is there EVER a time you cannot process the invoice for payment immediately after getting the paperwork together?" or "Does every invoice include all the appropriate information for processing each and every time?"

If a person is not cooperating, they may respond with something like "most of the time", or "hardly ever do I have an issue". This sort of "non-quantifiable" answer warrants deeper questioning.

When you are finished documenting the reality (current state) using Post-it® notes as shown in Figure 5, you are now ready to add a time line to the process.

Note: this is a simplified example. Even so, there are many other possible types of waste that can be preventing your company from turning the key to auto-matching.

Putting time values on the process map

Of course, you can just ask the clerk how much time she spends. We already have an idea what she will say. On Figure 5, we've indicated the general belief that it takes about 3 minutes to process each invoice.

But our goal in this part of the kaizen is to get the true facts. Actual data. Better, the kaizen team should put this belief to the test. The best way to do this is through direct observation.

Doing time observations

Time observations (also called a time study) are especially important for accurately measuring the work load at the area or machine that is the focus of the kaizen. A time observation captures all the steps that were recorded on the current state chart and the cycle time for each task separately.

In this section we will observe Kim while she processes a batch of 20 invoices.

Because time observations take place where and while the work is happening, they are also useful to verify the sequence of events and make adjustments to the team's documentation of the current state.

Figure 8 shows a sample blank time observation sheet that CCI uses.

There are many instances when it's not practical to do a time observation for one unit, in this case "one invoice." Kim rarely processes just one invoice at a time. She instead groups them for processing, because to process invoices one at a time from start to finish would not be practical.

NO.	Component Task	1	2	3	4	5	6	7	8	9	10	Component Task time	Points Observed
1													
2													
3													
4													
5													
6													
7													
8													
9													
11													
12													
10													
13													
14													
TIME FOR 1 CYCLE													

Figure 8 - Blank Time Observation Sheet

For this part of the process, generally it's best to go to the place where the actual work is performed, which is Kim's work area. This visit can be planned in advance to give the person time to prepare.

Ask the clerk to perform the functions of the job that were documented earlier in the event. As she performs the steps, one or more of the team members should be writing down each step of the task in detail.

Then transfer each step of the process you observed during observation into the column labeled "component task" of the Time Observation Sheet.

As you do this take some time to think about the approximate time it might take for each step. Estimating this can be tricky. You want to write down tasks that can actually be measured; it's a balancing act. The team wants achieve a detailed understanding of the process. But too much minute detail will be very difficult to capture. For example, don't try to time a step such as "Press enter on the key board." Look for opportunities to describe the activities so they include just enough detail.

Next, select three team members to perform the time study.

When everyone's ready, ask the A/P clerk to take the team to her work area.

Materials and equipment needed:

    A stop watch

    Clip boards

    The Time Observation Sheet

    Relevant Diagram/Floor Plan (for recording movement)

    Paper and Pencils

The observation group

Make-up of the Time Observation Group

Time Keeper	Time Recorder	Map Recorder
• Operates the stop watch	• Records the observed times	• Creates the standard work sheet

Figure 9 Observation Group Roles

Time keeper duties: using the stop watch

You'll notice columns on the Time Observation Sheet marked 1 through 13. Each numbered column represents a separate time observation. Observed times are recorded down the sheet.

The Team Leader can make a judgment call depending on the variability in the process whether it's necessary to record many observations. High variability requires more time observations in order to capture a good average. You should time low variability processes at least twice.

Know your stopwatch! All great chefs know their tools. They will never stop in the middle of baking a cake to go find and read the instructions for how to use the oven.

Each stop watch is different, so be sure to read the instructions before you begin making observations. If it's complicated, you might want to practice.

When using the stop watch it's easier to call out the total elapsed time as you reach each new step, rather than resetting the stop watch to zero after each step, then going back later and calculating the individual time for each step.

If you are using the method we think works best, don't hesitate to pause (temporarily stop the watch) and stop the person doing the work (in our case Kim) if you think you didn't capture the time correctly at any point. You will be focusing not only on the tasks actively done, but also the time between tasks.

Time recorder duties: writing the time for each process element

On the 'Time Observation Sheet' there are two boxes in each column, one on top of the other. The top box is where the time for each step is written, and the bottom box is for the total elapsed time.

The Time Keeper will be calling out the total (cumulative) elapsed time as the clerk performs each step. It's easiest and accurate to record the total elapsed time in the bottom box. You can go back afterwards and do the math to calculate the individual time for each process element.

When you're finished, the Time Observation will look something like Figure 10.

Time Observation Sheet

Project Area / Machine: Batch of 20 invoices   Date: _____

NO.	Component Task	1	2	3	4	5	6	7	8	9	10	Component Task time	Points Observed
1	Go get mail from inbox	60 / 60	65 / 65	63 / 63	59 / 59	61 / 61	61 / 61	60 / 60	63 / 63	62 / 62	60 / 60	61	Note: front desk clerk already separated raw material from expense invoices
2	Open Mail & review information on invoice.	835 / 895	870 / 935	820 / 883	845 / 904	845 / 906	850 / 911	840 / 900	875 / 938	790 / 852	796 / 856	837	This step is combined with step one on the current state map.
3	Look in file to find appropriate packing slips/PO's	180 / 1075	305 / 1240	191 / 1074	201 / 1105	512 / 1418	413 / 1324	181 / 1081	195 / 1133	212 / 1064	218 / 1074	261	The receiving clerk attaches the PO to the packing slip.
4	Match packing slips/PO's with invoices - mark those that don't.	1540 / 2615	1596 / 2836	1510 / 2584	1533 / 2638	1575 / 2993	1450 / 2774	1600 / 2681	1450 / 2583	1602 / 2666	1540 / 2614	1540	This step is combined with step 3 above on the current state map.
5	Is the PO# on the invoice?	410 / 3025	420 / 3256	421 / 3005	411 / 3049	415 / 3408	416 / 3190	415 / 3096	411 / 2994	412 / 3078	400 / 3014	413	
6	If a PO # is missing, physically find buyer for PO#.	2850 / 5875	690 / 3946	3800 / 6805	0 / 3049	0 / 3408	1910 / 5100	420 / 3516	0 / 2994	4200 / 7278	0 / 3014	1387	Kim does not wait for the missing PO#. She will track down any of the buyers or purchasing mgr.
7	If invoice does not match the pkg slip quantity received, contact receiving and/or supplier.	0 / 5875	1296 / 5242	0 / 6805	0 / 3049	0 / 3408	1010 / 6110	0 / 3516	0 / 2994	0 / 7278	0 / 3014	231	Kim generally contacts receiving to double check what was recevied, and then contacts the supplier if receiving was correct.
8	Wait for Receiving to confirm or correct.	0 / 5875	5255 / 10497	0 / 6805	0 / 3049	0 / 3408	6200 / 12310	0 / 3516	0 / 2994	0 / 7278	0 / 3014	1146	
9	If invoice price does not match the PO price, contact the buyer.	725 / 6600	0 / 10497	1202 / 8007	1110 / 4159	0 / 3408	750 / 13060	1060 / 4576	905 / 3899	0 / 7278	950 / 3964	670	This step is combined with step 7 on the current state map.
10	Wait for Buyer to correct invoice	8350 / 14950	0 / 10497	8300 / 16307	16900 / 21059	0 / 3408	6600 / 19660	5200 / 9776	7450 / 11349	0 / 7278	7750 / 11714	6055	
11	Process for payment	2650 / 17600	2720 / 13217	2710 / 19017	2715 / 23774	2690 / 6098	2692 / 22352	2702 / 12478	2705 / 14054	2705 / 9983	2706 / 14420	2700	
12													
13													
	TIME FOR 1 CYCLE in minutes	293.3	220.3	316.95	396.23	102	372.53	208	234.2	166	240.3	255	In Minutes

Figure 10 CCI's Recorded Time Observations

Map recorder duties: creating the standard work sheet (spaghetti diagram)

Use the relevant floor plan/diagram to create the 'standard work sheet.' You will draw (record) the travel distance for each step performed away from the immediate work area. Make multiple arrows, to indicate how many trips are made. The arrows indicate the direction of travel.

In our example, the Map Recorder draws an arrow on the floor plan for each time Kim steps away from her work area. There may be valid and varied reasons for stepping away from the

> **Wasted Motion** is one of Lean's Seven Types of Deadly Waste.
>
> Wasted motion impedes flow and adds no value to the process.
>
> (See *Non-Stock Production* by Shigeo Shingo, Productivity Press, Cambridge, MA 1988)

work area. Some examples may be to get the mail, investigate an issue or to file.

It's important to get this right. Analyzing the Standard Work Sheet reveals whether the work area is right-located, meaning located closest to other areas most relevant to the overall process. It also provides invaluable information about the Current State that informs the kaizen team's work toward the Future State.

CCI's team Map Recorder created what you see in Figure 11.

What we're after is accuracy. It's not an artistic competition. In fact, the worse this drawing looks, the more waste is revealed. This creates an opportunity to make even more improvements!

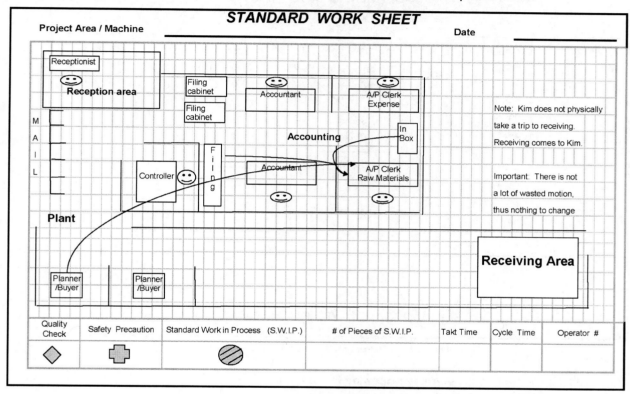

Figure 11 Results of CCI's Travel Observations

Create the time line

Even a great chef sometimes gets it wrong. She looks at a recipe disaster, understands what went wrong, and works to make improvements.

Similarly, after the CCI team finished its time observations, they found out their original assumptions were off the mark.

Knowing this will get them ready to begin working out improvements. They will be working from <u>real</u> information.

Next, based on actual observations, the team prepares a time line and adds it to the bottom of the current state map. This is the cycle time of the process.

> **Cycle time = Time to complete the process. Do not include wait time**

Each step is separated and the time to process each step is written below the line. Write processing time below the line and wait time above.

This is a standard way to do this. You may have your own method. No matter how, use a method that separates processing time from wait time.

Be sure to label the batch size on the current state map.

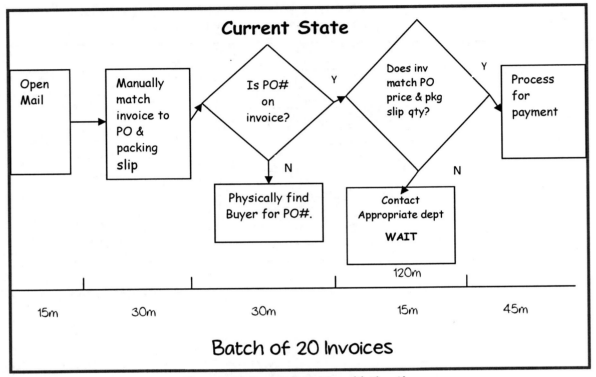

Figure 12 CCI Current State Map with Time Line

The results of the time study were **eye-opening** for the team.

So what do the results (Figure 12) mean?

First off, they found out their initial ideas about processing cycle time were far off the mark.

When the kaizen team created the A3 "Initial State" (see Figure 5), they believed the cycle time to process an invoice was approximately 3 minutes. As a result of their time observations, they learned the process really takes a bit under 7 minutes per invoice or (135 minutes for a batch of 20.)

They also saw clearly how much waste was bogging the process down. They now had a good basis for figuring out what to do to improve it.

The team learned clearly how time observations provide a way to calculate waste. One way to calculate waste is to compare the wasted time observed to the average number of invoices processed in a specific time period. In this example, let's assume the unit of measure is one day.

> **CCI's Current State** cycle time was thought to be 3 minutes. It's actually 6.75 minutes!

Takt time

What is takt time? Takt time is the rate of demand coming into a process. This is a concept that's very familiar to lean operations people. They work all the time to synchronize operations to the rate of customer demand. Support people sometimes need help understanding what their "customer" demand is.

> **Takt time = Net available Working minutes ÷ required output**

The CCI team has to figure out how well Kim was keeping up with A/P demand. She has to process an average of 500 invoices/week with a normal work week being 35 hours, taking into consideration breaks and lunches.

If you convert 35 hours into minutes, you have a 2100-minute work week.

This means an invoice needs to be processed every 4.2 minutes (2100/500) in order to meet customer demand.

The kaizen team next analyzed the time line to determine if the A/P process could meet customer demand in the current state. They calculated Kim was actually processing an invoice every 6.75 minutes. That's a problem!

Something has to give.

The company needs either to add an additional A/P clerk, or the kaizen team needs to figure out how to remove some time from the process. That means getting rid of waste.

Day 2

The task today is to design the Ideal process. The team will answer this question: what would the process look like if everything was perfect?

Document the ideal state

This is the best part of any kaizen, and also the toughest!

When the team is developing the ideal state, be clear to the team that an "ideal state" is most likely something that will not be achieved through this single event.

Now that they see the problems, they will be impatient to start fixing. This is a good time to review the Diagnostic. It's an opportunity to show the team the bigger picture. Take time to review the continuum from traditional through necessary intermediate and advances stages, to complete lean management. It's an incremental process, and any given kaizen is one increment.

This may be a challenge to the team at CCI. They are starting from a manual process, thus this one kaizen most likely will not lead the team to Lean Management. They need to realize this kaizen the start of a journey.

Think about it this way. When the kaizen succeeds, improvements will happen. That's the point! The team will rightly be proud of what they've done.

But the team needs a clear picture of the road ahead, so improvements can continue.

Jane helped the team understand that "continuous improvement is a way of life." She used the Diagnostic as a way to show how mature Lean Management will look.

Ok....so it's not likely this kaizen team will create the ideal state. In fact, we would not recommend leaping ahead too far anyway, unless robust lean controls are in place and working well. We cannot lose control of the business.

Future events, where we build success upon success, will get us closer and closer.

CCI's team was less likely to get frustrated when only a small improvement is achieved, because Jane showed them the big picture.

Time to get out the Post-it® notes!

To create the Ideal State Map, Jane took the kaizen team through a similar process used for the current state map.

Jane started in a good spot: she asked the team to look at the current state and eliminate all the rework or non-value added steps.

This was a difficult concept for CCI's people. They needed to be educated about what rework or non-value-added means applied to their work. Kim argued that some current state work, such as "is the PO# or requestor name on the invoice" is normal, not "rework."

Jane challenged the group by reminding them that we're not trying to come up with a solution at this point. In an ideal situation, why wouldn't the PO# be on the invoice?

Give the team ample time to develop the new process. Here's what they came up with.

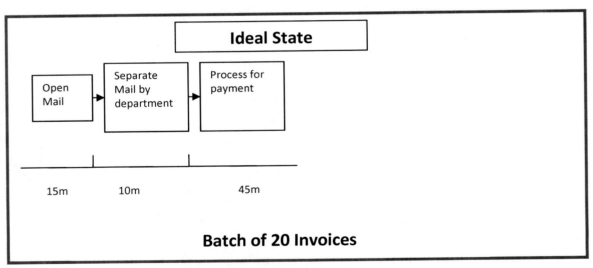

Figure 13 CCI's "Ideal State" Map

Notice that the parts of the process that represented waste in the current state were removed from the ideal state. Also notice the cycle time difference between the current and ideal state.

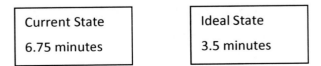

That's a 48% improvement!

Remember, when documenting the ideal state, The Team Leader keeps the team from coming up with solutions. We're just looking for ideas at this point.

One important comment: If you look at the Diagnostic, you will notice that ideally there is no invoice when you get to advanced stages of lean. "Autopay" eliminates the need for an invoice. Even though autopay should ultimately be the "ideal state", it's something beyond the thought process of this team at this stage of lean. In their mind, the ideal state is what's shown above. And that's okay.

Jane made a decision at this point to aim the team at something they can accomplish now. Jane knows CCI's people are in the beginning stages of lean. Many times, people new to lean cannot fathom a "true" ideal state. As they learn more, they will see more and more opportunities for improvement.

Now it's time to brainstorm!

Brainstorm improvements

Now you can turn the team loose generating ideas for how to fix the observed problems.

I can almost guarantee this exercise will be difficult for some team members because it will take them out of their comfort zone and force them to think of ideas that would normally never enter their mind.

Remember, this team is going from a very manual paper process to a fully automated system. This can be a very tough transition. A good structured brainstorming session will help get their thinking going.

Conducting the brainstorming session

This is an exercise that is done individually.

With the Current State and the Ideal State maps posted in the kaizen room, Jane asks each team member to come up with at least one, but preferable two or more ideas for each of the areas of waste.

In other words, ask the team to focus on the areas of waste that were removed from the current state to create from the ideal state. Worded differently, "How can we get from where we are, to where we want to be?"

The Leader is responsible ahead of time for writing on a separate Large Post-it® Easel Pad, the areas of waste that are candidates for elimination. The leader is also responsible for developing a list of questions that, if answered, will lead the team to the ideal state. These questions should be worded in such a way that, if answered, will bring the process from the current to the ideal state. Some examples:

> How can we ensure the PO# will be listed on the invoice?
>
> How can we ensure the PO & quantity received always match the invoice?
>
> What's the easiest method for matching the PO to the invoice?

The areas of the current state that were removed from the ideal state are marked "WASTE."

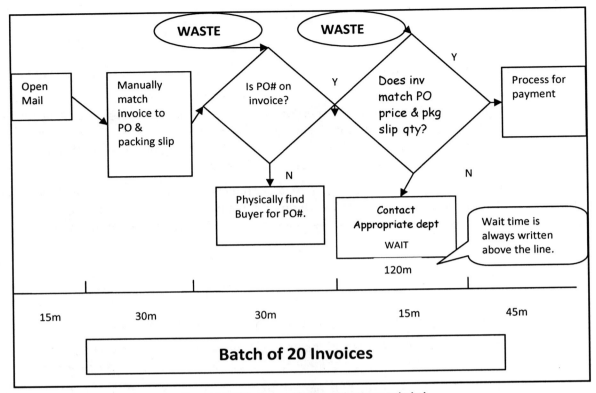

Figure 14 CCI's Current State with Waste Labeled

Ask each person to write ideas for eliminating "WASTE" as outlined above on a note.

They should use **one Post-it® note per idea**.

Ask them also to write the question # on each Post-it®. Do not put a name on the Post-it®, just the idea and question #.

Give the team plenty of time to come up with their answers. The amount of time the team should take to write their ideas depends on the number of questions and the complexity of the issues. Pay attention and ask the team if they are finished once you see that they've stopped writing and/or give you the impression they are finished.

Many times, members of the team are reluctant to come up with improvement ideas. It's your job as a leader to motivate the group to participate. You may consider coming up with one or two ideas of your own and presenting them to the group as an example. This may help jog their thought processes. You may also remind them that there are no "dumb" ideas. Every idea is valuable even if you don't know how to make it happen.

Make sure the members of the team understand that just because they come up with an idea, doesn't mean they will be responsible for making it happen.

Another important note: remind the group and also yourself to focus on the process, not on a particular person. In almost all instances, a well documented process with accountability attached almost always generates positive results.

> If people are following a well documented process, then it's the process that's broken. FIX THE PROCESS!

If people are not following a well documented process, then there are grounds for disciplinary action or training, depending on the situation.

Having said that, let's say that if it comes to light during the brainstorming session that a particular person is not following a well documented process, one idea may be to "Provide training to those that are not following the process."

When finished, the leader should gather the Post-it® notes and arrange them on the easel pad. The questions should be written at the top of the paper with the Post-it® notes underneath the appropriate question. The results of CCI's brainstorming session are shown on Figure 15.

Note: Figure 15 is a simplified example. Generally, there are many more ideas generated and posted on the easel pad.

1. How can we ensure the PO# will be listed on the invoice?	2. How can we ensure the PO Price & Qty received always match the invoice?	3. What's the easiest method for matching the PO to the invoice?
Q1. Return all invoices w/no PO# to the vendor with a note.	Q2. Train Rec clerks to receive the correct item# & qty into system.	Q3. Match from a receiving report.
Q1. Send a memo stating no payment unless the process is followed.	Q2. Train Receivers.	Q3. Print report in system that shows receipts & match from report.
Q1. Educate the vendors	Q2. Set a tolerance in the system to pay if the qty rec'd was plus/minus 10% of PO.	Q3. Have system automatically 3 way match. If no match, invoice goes on hold.
Q1. Train vendors	Q2. Set an acceptable tolerance level for qtys ordered (PO) vs. qtys. received	Q3. Use System to do 3 way match.
Q1. Educate buyers to properly fill out a PO w instructions to the supplier.	Q2. Train the buyers to input the correct qty and price on PO.	Q3. System shld know if receipt doesn't match inv. & put on hold or send out alert
Q1. Call vendor when invoice is received and tell them to re-send invoice with PO#.	Q2. Buyers should fill out PO correctly to avoid problems later.	Q3. Implement a "pay on receipt" system where there's no invoice involved.
Q1. Train buyers to correctly complete a purchase order.	Q2. Set up price list in system for all parts.	
	Q2. Set up price list in system for all purchased parts.	

Figure 15 CCI's Proposed Actions

The next step is a collaborative exercise.

With the team's input, the leader re-arranges the ideas into related groups.

This is what happened when Jane Holmes led the team through this procedure.

Jane: "It looks to me like these ideas pertain to buyers." She pulled the Post-it® about buyers' activities off the easel.

| Q1. Train buyers to correctly complete a purchase order. | Q1. Educate buyers to properly fill out a PO with instructions to the supplier. |

Jane continued, "It also appears the two ideas are similar, just worded differently. Do you agree to re-write both ideas on to one Post-it® similar like this?"

| Q1. Train buyers to properly complete a PO |

Once Jane had consensus, she rewrote the combined idea onto one Post-it® and discarded the others. She continued grouping similar ideas with the team's consensus. She encouraged the team to elaborate on their ideas and help combine them into similar buckets.

When Jane was finished, CCI's chart looked similar to the Figure 16.

1. How can we ensure the PO# will be listed on the invoice?	2. How can we ensure the PO price & Qty received always match the invoice?	3. What's the easiest method for matching the PO to the invoice?
Q1. Train vendors in the form of a memo stating co. policy for paying invoices	Q2. Train Rec clerks to receive the correct item# & qty into system.	Q3. Print report in system that shows receipts & match from report.
Q1. Train buyers to properly complete a PO	Q2. Set an acceptable tolerance level for qtys ordered (PO) vs. qtys rec'd	Q3. Use System to do 3 way match.
	Q2. Set up price list in system for all purchased parts.	Q3. Implement a "pay on receipt" system where there's no invoice involved.

Figure 16 CCI's Grouped Chart

Standard work

Before we go any further, it's important that the team understand the term "Standard Work" because it's used a lot in the rest of this cookbook. Revising the A/P process and creating new standard work that will lock in the improvements the kaizen team makes – this is what we are ultimately after.

Standard work is very similar to a procedure or standard operating process.

The main difference is that standard work is "time bound", meaning there is a time associated to complete each process. Standard work is also presented visually. It lays out the precise work sequence for completing a given work step or task.

Figure 17 in this book is an example of standard work. It's visual, shows the precise steps used. Put together with the team's time measurements, it's the standard work "base line" for Kim's A/P process.

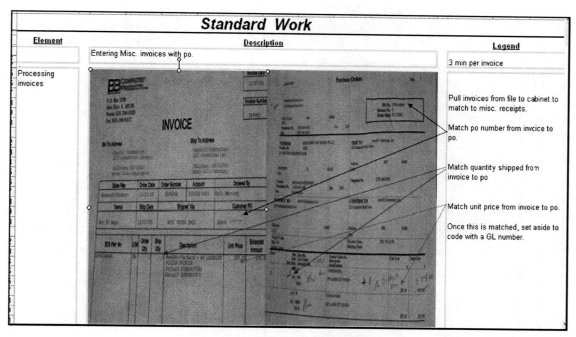

Figure 17 Example of Standard Work

The format for documenting standard work is unimportant. There are many variations to the formatting. Just think "Visual."

Benefit/Effort matrix

Once all brainstorming ideas are up on the board, the Kaizen team has to use some method for rating or prioritizing the ideas. For this, we use a Benefit/Effort matrix.

The Benefit/Effort matrix is a four-box chart that lets your team plot the effort involved in doing a project against the benefits that will result.

One axis represents "Effort", which includes all the negative aspects, such as time, cost, effort, risk, complexity, etc. associated with the idea.

The other 'Benefit'' axis represents all the positive aspects, such as revenue, cost-savings, and the risk of not doing it.

We make the left lower corner of each axis 'Low = 1' and the top and right of the axes 'High = 10'. Exact precision doesn't matter. The important thing is to show one item's difficulty and importance relative to another's.

This tool helps to focus yourself and the team on the impact each idea will have on achieving the target conditions of this kaizen event. The team is not charged with fixing everything! For example, if the ultimate target condition is to move a manual paper matching process to a computerized auto-match process, then any idea (even a good one) outside that scope will most likely not happen as a result of this kaizen event.

Figure 16 shows the layout of the Benefit/Effort matrix chart.

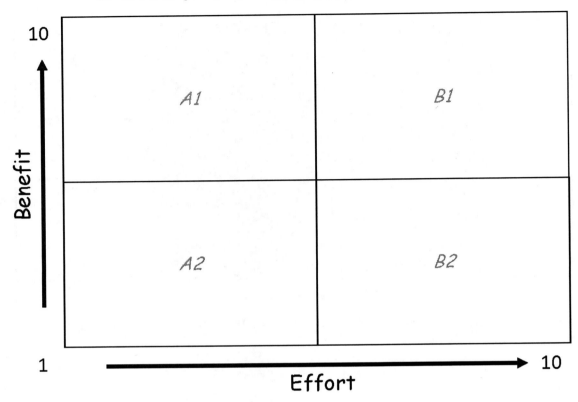

Figure 18 Blank Benefit / Effort Matrix

Prioritizing the team's ideas, then, involves placing the ideas within this matrix, so that each idea's intrinsic and relative value are visible to everybody.

We've made this easy by labeling the boxes as follows:

Box A1 = An idea involves minimal effort and is highly beneficial to the kaizen event success
  Typically can be complete during the event
Box A2 = An idea involves minimal effort and low impact to the kaizen event success
  Typically can be complete during the week, but make sure all A1s are complete first, leaving A2s if time permits
Box B1 = An idea involves a great deal of effort, but is highly beneficial to the kaizen event success
  Typically goes on a completion plan to be completed within the next 90 days
Box B2 = An idea involves a great deal of effort, and low impact to the project success
  These ideas probably should not be implemented because they require a great deal of effort and would not help reach the goals of the kaizen event

Placing the team's ideas on the grid requires judgment about whether an idea is harder or easier, more or less important, than the other items already plotted. The team leader's job is to make sure they're plotted roughly in the right position, relative to each other.

This is where having the right team involved in the kaizen event makes all the difference! The relevant process "owners" can decide how much benefit to assign a project. Technical people can help figure out how much effort a project will take.

As a good rule of thumb, the team can start by "cherry picking" the things that are obviously the easiest or hardest, and the most or least important. Plotting these in the four corners helps the team understand what you're doing and makes it easier to classify the rest of the stuff.

> Some teams come up with ideas that involve other people or groups not present during the kaizen.

If you're new at leading a team, it's very difficult to know what can be finished this week. When in doubt, classify as an A1. Rapid experiments done later will determine if the A1 should be moved to a B1.

It is very important that whatever ideas the team comes up with are communicated to EVERYONE involved in that process.

For example, in a large company there may be ten A/P clerks and only four of them are present for the kaizen event.

The Team Leader makes sure the new ideas are communicated to the other six A/P clerks before the idea is implemented. One sure way of not getting buy-in from people is to give them new standard work for their job when they had no input into the process.

DO NOT UNDERESTIMATE THE IMPORTANCE OF THIS. It's also possible you may need approval from a manager as well. Make sure all areas of approval are covered. Larger companies are sometimes more difficult to get buy-in from all involved.

Plotting on the benefit/effort matrix

So now it's time to rate the Crumple Crunch kaizen team's ideas.

We begin by reviewing the grouped chart the team developed that summarizes their ideas addressed to each question. (See Figure 16) Addressing each of these three questions successfully will require action in a number of areas. Plotting them on the benefit/effort matrix helps decide what to do first, second, etc.

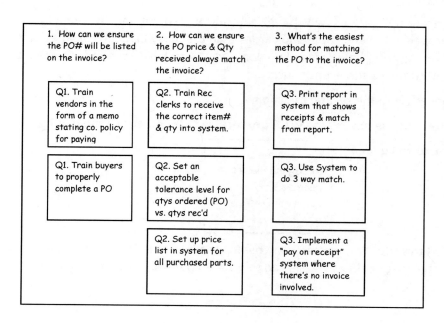

CCI's Office Kaizen Leader Jane led a discussion focused on each question and each idea. She started by posting a blank Benefit/Effort Matrix chart in the room.

Then Jane began with the first question, first idea.

Question #1 – How can we ensure the PO# will be listed on the invoice?

    1st brainstorming idea:

> Q1. Train vendors in the form of a memo stating co. policy for paying

After a short discussion, the team decided that composing and sending a memo to all suppliers would be easy to do. They believed it can be done within one week.

The team assigned a rating of A1 to Idea #1

Jane moved Idea#1/Question#1 from the idea chart and placed it in the A1 box on the Benefit/Effort Matrix. She then moved on to the next idea.

    2nd brainstorming idea:

> Q1. Train buyers to properly complete a PO

In this case, it's imperative that POs are written accurately and completely.

This one idea/issue will have a big impact on the project success.

This places the idea somewhere in the upper half (A1 or B1) of the matrix.

But at this point the team was not sure just how much work or effort would be involved. The team went back and forth on the issue for a while and decided to place the Idea#1/Question#2 in the A1 box. For the time being ...

When in doubt, it's best to pick A1, which typically indicates something is an idea that can be completed during the kaizen week. If it ends up being harder than originally planned, the idea can be moved to the B1 area and put on the completion plan. You don't want it to fall off the radar screen, because it is actually important to the kaizen event's success.

The CCI team moved on to the second question.

Question #2 – How can we ensure the PO & qty received always match the invoice?

    1st brainstorming idea:

> Q2. Train Receiving clerks to receive the correct item# & qty into system.

The team handled this situation the same as training the buyers in Question#1, except now it's directed toward training receiving clerks. They agreed this item belonged in the A1 quadrant.

Question #2 – How can we ensure the PO & qty received always match the invoice?

    2nd brainstorming idea:
> Q2. Set an acceptable tolerance level for qtys ordered (PO) vs. qtys rec'd

Setting tolerance levels can be tricky, but it's but very important to A/P, as well as other departments, especially Production. Depending on expertise of the company, this item could fall within the A1 or B1 category. Again, the team was unsure, so they rated the idea an A1. They decided it could be changed later if necessary.

Because knowledge about tolerance levels among the team was not clear, they decided further study was needed before the team could assign a meaningful rating. They understood that If the explanation becomes too time consuming, the training on tolerance levels could be handled by Rapid Experiments (later in this cookbook.)

Question #2 – How can we ensure the PO & qty received always matches the invoice?

    3rd brainstorming idea:
> Q2. Set up price list in system for all purchased parts.

The ability to set up a price list for all purchased parts will depend on whether CCI's software system can handle it, and whether resources are available to do it. The team had to decide what benefit and effort are involved if a price list is set up.

Suppose the team agrees that once a price list is set up, it will help automate the PO process and support implementing kanbans where no PO is used. Doing this would also help facilitate pay-on-receipt processing in the future.

After some discussion, the team concludes that implementing a price list might require a lot more thought and effort involving many different functional areas within CCI. Everybody agreed: doing this would be a huge benefit to the success of the project and would allow for future growth. They rated this item B1 to be done within the next 90 days.

Question #3 – What's the easiest method for matching the PO to the invoice?

    1st brainstorming idea:
> Q3. Print report in system that shows receipts & match from report.

It seemed to the CCI team that the person who submitted this idea had some working knowledge of how the computer system works. How else could they come up with this idea?

Before making a decision, it would help if the team could get more information and some more details from the person who came up with the idea.

Jane asked for a more thorough explanation. Joe from IT and Kim explained in detail as follows:

A three-way manual match is when the purchase order, packing slip (used by receiving), and the invoice are matched for quantity and price.

The receiving report (which is a report generated from the packing slips that were received into the system), is exactly the same information that is needed to match the paper packing slip to the invoice – FOR QTY ONLY. Generally, prices are not on a packing slip.

It's just much easier to use a receiving report to match quantity received, rather than to chase down all the original packing slips, sort them, and look for the pertinent information.

There should be no difference between the two unless the clerk who enters the information makes a mistake in which case we can manually pull the packing slip and do a three-way manual match on an exception basis.

This is an easier method than pulling all packing slips and doing a manual match for every invoice.

The team agreed this is a good interim option until the system is set up to do automated three-way match.

The team decided that Kim (AP Clerk) should time the process both ways for a specified time period. No matter what, this will be helpful when documenting the time saved once the new process is in place.

The team decided to post this idea in A1 quadrant. If it turns out this idea doesn't pass the audit test or save the A/P clerk time, then it can be discarded entirely.

Question #3 – What's the easiest method for matching the PO to the invoice?

2nd brainstorming idea: Q3. Use System to do 3 way match.

Jane, the team leader, explained that while this is the goal of this kaizen event, immediately jumping into using the system to three-way match cannot be started until all the other ideas in the A1 quadrant are complete. If proper training for all operations that affect A/P is not done, using the system to match may actually cause errors, such as over/under payment. In particular, it is imperative proper tolerance levels are set in place before turning the switch to auto-matching.

That said, the team concluded it is appropriate to move this idea to B1. It is obvious that moving to auto-match is essential to the success of this project, but may take a bit longer than a week to complete.

Question #3 – What's the easiest method for matching the PO to the invoice?

3rd brainstorming idea: Q3. Implement a "pay on receipt" system where there's no invoice involved.

The CCI kaizen team gave this idea some thought.

A pay-on-receipt system implies an advanced stage of lean with mature controls in place throughout the value stream. With pay-on-receipt, there is NO invoice. The computer system automatically pays based on the receipt. This is using a completely automated system without much human intervention.

Jane knew that Robby Gunner, CCI's Lean Coordinator, was already talking up the operational benefits of doing this. In fact, Jane also knew (as stated earlier in this kaizen) that the team did not account for this in the ideal state. Robby must have already talked to IT about autopay because she doubts anyone else on the team would think of this advanced idea.

While this could be a great opportunity for breakthrough change at CCI, yielding many benefits, the team needs to be cautious. Complete automation would be risky if implemented prematurely and if the necessary controls are not in place. As an accountant, Jane understood that she and the kaizen team had broad and important responsibility for making sure the company's accounting and management controls were strong.

Imagine that the team automated this process immediately. What would happen?

Jane asked the group to think about all the waste in the current processes and how that may affect automation.

The team discussed the current situation where there are ingoing issues with invoices not always matching the PO. In such instances, automating the payment process could potentially cause errors. Invoices could be paid at an incorrect price or quantity. The rework involved to correct such mistakes is substantial and costly. One look at the current state map showed this is already the case within the current process. Putting in pay-on-receipt too soon could result in overpayments and underpayments. Underpayments could result in lost discounts.

Bottom line: the team decided this is an excellent opportunity for a future kaizen, but only after all training on the "Completion Plan" has taken place, AND the company is using the system to auto three-way match for some period of time, with few or no problems.

Today, however, the immediate issues should be corrected first. Once a solid process is in place that is working flawlessly, that's the time to think about more automation.

Additionally, doing pay-on-receipt seemed outside of the scope of the current kaizen event.

The CCI team concluded they can accomplish their current goals without pay-on-receipt.

They placed this idea in the B2 quadrant.

Figure 19 shows the team's results.

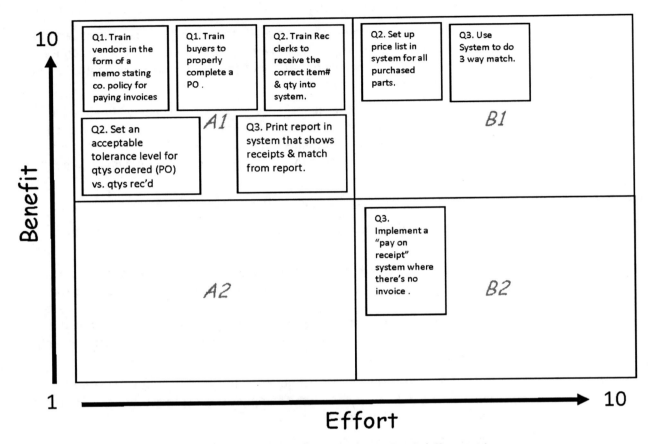

Figure 19 CCI's Completed Benefit/Effort Matrix

 Days 3 & 4

Rapid experiments

First a few words about "rapid experiments."

When organizations are trying to effect changes, there is tension built into the process of managing change. Some people want to "table-top" any innovation through endless discussion, which seems to go nowhere slowly. Others want to plunge ahead a "just do it" even if it means wasting resources on changes that don't always work and need to be reworked.

Rapid Experiments (or Rapid Experimentation) offer a way to speed up decision making while improving the chances that the changes tried will actually work.

Rapid Experiments let your team try out their changes and apply disciplined methods to measure the results quickly and accurately. The team can test some of the ideas; meet with others in the organization to get their feel for some of the ideas; and implement some of the ideas that can be finished during the week of the event.

Successful kaizen will always result in putting change into action!

Now for the fun part!

It's time to make change happen ... it's a good idea to have a camera handy to take before and after pictures of the improvements you're about to make!

But wait! So you have a Benefit/Effort Matrix with all sorts of ideas posted. What next?

Imagine you are a beginning cook in a restaurant. The executive chef brings you a copy of the menu and says, "This is what we are making today."

It can be overwhelming and sometimes it's hard to decide what tasks to focus on first. Break the eggs, chop the vegetables, toss the salad?

You need help getting started.

This is the situation CCI's kaizen team found themselves in after they had completed their Benefit/Effort Matrix. (Figure 19)

With Jane Holmes' guidance, the team decided to begin with the ideas in the upper left quadrant – A1 – of the Benefit/Effort Matrix. Was this cherry-picking? No! By selecting projects doable during the kaizen week, the team was actually getting something meaningful done while learning.

Remember, CCI's team had Joe Johnson, an IT support person, on the team. The kaizen week provided an excellent opportunity to make use of IT expertise. In many companies it's often rare to have the undivided attention of an IT person for an entire week.

In this author's experience, many companies start with the upper left quadrant of the Benefit/Effort Matrix. These ideas have potentially high impact, plus they are possible to attain during the kaizen week.

Items falling within the B1 quadrant (autopay for example) can be taken out of the current kaizen's immediate to 90-day action plan and put in the B2 area.

Generally B2 ideas are not necessary to the success of the current event. Keep in mind we are not saying these ideas are not important at all.

We are only saying it's not important to the success of the current event. Such ideas will come up again in more advanced stages of lean, and may then fall within future 90-day action plans.

Some companies prefer to keep these ideas in a so-called "parking lot." This is a way of saying that important ideas will be addressed later, just not right now. It's been the authors experience, however, that "parking lot" items come up again on their own in future events because they are truly important, not because they were placed in the "parking lot."

It's a good idea for the team leader to refer to the Ideal State as a goal that the company will attain in its lean journey.

Doing rapid experiments

To get started, the team went back to the benefit/effort matrix and looked again at the ideas.

For this process, they started out by discussing each of the ideas again and developing a plan of action for rapid experimentation.

Beginning with the first idea in A1 Quadrant:

> Q1. Train vendors in the form of a memo stating co. policy for paying invoices

The team worked together to decide what information should be included in the memo to the vendors. They consulted the Purchasing Manager, Stacy Stiletto, to get her input as well.

Typically, vendors will comply with a reasonable company policy. Remember…this is a partnership, especially in a lean company.

The memo they drafted included verbiage similar to the following: "to ensure on time payment, all invoices sent to Crumple Crunch Industries must include our purchase order number. This is the only method we have to match the invoice to our records."

Some companies also include additional statements such as the following: "please accept only faxed or e-mailed purchase orders using Crumple Crunch Industries' standard purchase order form. Verbal purchase orders will not be accepted. A copy of our company's purchase order format is attached." This will help tighten internal controls. Kathy Anderson, CCI's Controller was on board with this.

A manager might have to determine if it's reasonable to inform the vendor that all invoices will be returned without proper information and whether this verbiage should be communicated through the memo being drafted.

This should be a management decision. There might be some pushback from people within the company to send back invoices for corrections. This could cause invoices to get put on hold and possibly risk the vendor stopping deliveries. Production operations might be impacted. A managers needs to decide whether the problem is severe enough to force the issue and whether these outweigh the potential benefits.

CCI decided to send a few select team members to work on the memo and get help from the Purchasing Manager and others in the Purchasing Department.

Note: keep a copy or pictures of this letter to use for your presentation.

Assuming this letter is written and sent to all vendors during the event, there is no need to add it to the completion plan. Additionally, the Post-it® note for that idea can be removed from the Benefit/Effort matrix and marked complete.

The second idea in A1 Quadrant:

> Q1. Train buyers to properly complete a PO

As the leader, Jane informs the team that training employees (as opposed to vendors outside the company) requires written standard work.

She also reminded the team that processing improvements should get down to the root cause of the problem.

Standard work written for buyers would include instructions for properly filling out and submitting a purchase order to the vendor. Standard work is supposed to be followed.

Accounting should not have to pick up the pieces for areas of the organization that choose not to follow a process. Countermeasures for those instances will be reviewed later in this book.

The kaizen team needs to understand whether it will be difficult to work with the buyers to understand the process, and write standard work accordingly? Will the buyers cooperate with changing their standard work? How much input will they require?

Depending on the situation, training buyers might require its own kaizen event, especially in larger companies where there are sometimes many specialized buyers who are possibly located in other locations.

The team needs to decide if this is something the team can accomplish within the current event or with a meeting sometime in the near future. Having John, a buyer, in the kaizen event helps the team decide if this is a matter of having no standard work (so the team would have to start from scratch) or of fixing a few flaws in the buyers' standard work.

With John's assistance, the team decided a future kaizen event would be required. John did, however, agree to begin making sure the price is correct on the purchase order before the invoice gets to the A/P Clerk. He will also convey this message to the other buyer. John won't write standard work just yet because there are other issues that need to be addressed in their area that will be covered during the event. This event made him think of all the improvements he would like to make – but he will save his ideas for the future event.

The team believed it was feasible to schedule this event within the next two months.

It is still the responsibility of someone on the team to make sure this event is scheduled and completed. Scheduling the event will make its way to the completion plan as explained in the next section.

The third idea in A1 Quadrant:

> Q2. Train Rec clerks to receive the correct item# & qty into system.

The kaizen team decided to handle this situation the same as training the buyers.

In this case, however, the receiving clerks already have standard work.

During the event selected team members went to the receiving department and reviewed the standard work, made whatever corrections were necessary and trained the receiving clerks in using the updated standard work.

Remember, simply changing standard work does not ensure it will be followed. Most of us are experts at our job and do not open the standard work book on a daily basis.

If revising the standard work and training is not finished before the end of the event, it will go on the completion plan as a follow up. In this instance, CCI had the receiving clerk on the team. This made it possible to address this idea and complete it during the kaizen.

The fourth idea in A1 Quadrant:

> Q2. Set an acceptable tolerance level for qty's ordered (PO) vs. qty's rec'd

In this instance, the team should decide what's an acceptable level of tolerance when there is a discrepancy between the purchase order quantity and the received quantity.

In some industries, particularly manufacturing, there are legitimate reasons for discrepancies. MRO supplies such as nuts and bolts, bulk item like pellets and grain are examples. In these types of situations, a certain level of tolerance might be acceptable.

Tolerance levels, if set up properly, will stop an invoice from being paid if it's only outside what is considered "tolerable by the company."

Most computerized systems have the option of setting up several types of tolerance levels similar to the following:

Invoice price per piece = system can be set up to prevent or warn the user from entering an invoice when the price per piece on the invoice is a "specified percent" over and/or under the PO price per piece.

Total invoice price = system can be set up to prevent or warn the user from entering an invoice when the total price on the invoice is a "specified percent" over and/or under the total PO price.

Quantity received = system can be set up to prevent or warn the user from receiving a quantity where the quantity received is a "specified percent" over and/or under the PO quantity.

Quantity on Invoice = system can be set up to prevent or warn the user from entering an invoice where the quantity on the invoice is a "specified percent" over and/or under the quantity received.

In case the kaizen team does not understand the idea of tolerance levels, you might give the following example:

A company has the tolerance levels set up as follows
(all criteria must be met for any given invoice)

Invoice price per piece = tolerance set to allow 3% over PO price per piece

Total invoice price = tolerance set to reject an invoice >$1000 over PO total price

Quantity received = tolerance set to reject an invoice >10% over PO quantity ordered.

Quantity on Invoice = Must equal quantity received.

If the A/P clerk for that same company is processing an invoice with the following information:

Invoice	100,000 pieces at $.50 a piece	Total invoice: $50,000
PO	95,000 pieces at $.49 a piece	Total PO: $46,550
Received	95,000 pieces	

Should the invoice be paid without further approval? (Remember, <u>all</u> criteria must be met.)

Invoice price per piece = this setting allows 3% over PO price per piece and the difference between $.49 & $.50 is only 2% = **YES, pay this invoice**

Total invoice price = the tolerance is set to disallow >$1000 over PO total price and the total difference between the invoice & the PO is $3,450 = **NO, don't pay this invoice**

Quantity received = the tolerance is set not to allow >10% over PO quantity ordered and the total received is less than the quantity ordered = **YES, pay this invoice**

Quantity on Invoice = the tolerance is set so that invoice quantity must equal quantity received, the quantity received was 95,000 = **NO, don't pay this invoice.**

Jane used more examples until everyone on the team understood.

CCI's A/P kaizen team needed input from the areas directly involved in raw materials planning, buying and receiving before making a decision.

The team sent specified members to meet with appropriate people to determine if it's feasible to set the tolerances to specified values, what the tolerance values should be, and whether this should be done during the kaizen week.

The team worked with management and appropriate departments directly involved (i.e. Receiving, A/P, and Purchasing) during the event and came up with tolerance values for all criteria above.

They didn't, however, have an opportunity to investigate what steps are necessary to change the tolerances within the computer system or to fully understand the system's capabilities. More due diligence was needed from appropriate departments (i.e. IT, Purchasing, Operations) before such changes could be implemented.

A follow up on the completion plan was necessary.

The fifth idea in A1 Quadrant:

> Q3. Print report in system that shows receipts & match from report.

The team thought this idea was a great option. Using this report in the interim while the system is not set up to auto-match will really help.

Selected people on the kaizen team, particularly the Accounting Manager and Kim, the A/P clerk, should do some testing.

Additionally, they decided to go back to the current state map and look at the cycle time found for manual three-way matching. They believed they could directly and empirically measure any improvement in the cycle time. If no time was saved, then obviously this would not be a good option. The team guessed there would be time savings and this is a great interim option.

The team went back to the current state map. The cycle time to manually match the invoice to the purchase order and packing was listed as 30 minutes for a batch of 20.

| Using report to match 5.75 minutes | Current State 6.75 minutes | The team's time observation revealed a cycle time of 10 minutes when the report is used to match instead of the actual packing slips and purchase orders. |

That is an average time savings of 20 minutes per batch of 20 invoices.

At 500 invoices per week, that saves 500 minutes or over 8 hours

That's a 15% improvement!

This author would say that is an excellent interim step, especially if this is accomplished during the kaizen week.

The first idea in the B1 Quadrant:

> Q2. Set up price list in system for all purchased parts.

The ability to set up a price list for all purchased parts will depend on the capabilities of the software system and the resources available to implement and maintain the price list. The team should decide what benefit and effort is involved if a price list is set up.

The team leader should also mention that there are other things to consider. Some examples are listed below:

> Would part numbers need to be set up and maintained? If yes, what about one time purchases? Another method for price approval should be developed for non-standard purchases.
>
> Will the price list be maintained within the inventory system or as a separate system?
>
> What is the approval process for accepting price increases?
>
> Do some suppliers offer price breaks?
>
> Supplier maintenance....who will be responsible and what will be the process?

The above questions are only a few of many that may be relevant to the type of organization and the technology available. The point is that the leader should have the ability to think outside the scope of the event and ask questions that may have an impact on the process.

It would appear from the example above that implementing a price list may require a lot of thought and effort by many different areas. It does, however, have a huge benefit to the success of the project. Members of the team can go speak with the appropriate personnel to determine exactly what effort is involved.

After speaking with the appropriate personnel it was decided the purchasing manager (Stacy Stiletto) can get this done within the next 60 days. Since this process will not be completed before the end of the event, it will be added to the completion plan with Stacy Stiletto being responsible for its completion. Make sure Stacy knows this follow up will be on the completion plan and that she is responsible for making sure it's complete within the time frame above.

The second idea in the B1 Quadrant:

> Q3. Use System to do 3 way match.

Using the system to do the three-way match, if you recall, is listed as a target condition on the A3. Obviously it is a main indicator of the event's success.

You cannot do a rapid experiment specifically to this idea because it's dependent upon finishing all ideas in the A1 quadrant, specifically setting the tolerance levels.

The great news is that once the system is three-way auto-matching, the ideal state will be in place! The cycle time for processing an invoice will be reduced from the current state of 135 minutes for a batch of 20 to only 70 minutes!

That's almost a 50% reduction in cycle time. Imagine what CCI can do with that extra time!

Setting the tolerance levels should be 1st on the priority list, and then automatic three-way match is possible.

The only idea in the B2 Quadrant:

> Q3. Implement a "pay on receipt" system where there's no invoice.

As mentioned earlier, we cannot do any rapid experiments on this idea since we have a lot of work ahead of us first.

Rapid experiments wrap up

The leader must let the team finish the rapid experiments and re-cap what's complete. Keep track by marking "complete" on the Post-it® notes.

Some important words of advice

Most improvements are made in increments.

> It is not necessary, nor is it a good idea to build Rome in a day. It is, however, very important to build good, solid systems (even if they are manual) that will accommodate improvements later. Never get backed into a corner. And never think systems will solve all your problems. Any error is an opportunity to learn and improve. Never let errors slide by.

Here is an example:

> Let's say (for the sake of this example) you are a buyer for expense items such as office supplies, janitorial supplies, etc. Each day you place several purchase orders using the software system the company has instructed you to use, then you pass them on for approval by your manager.

> Now let's say your manager notices that in many instances you are using an incorrect account number. Instead of informing you and giving you an opportunity to improve, your manager just changes the account number each time.

> Your manager believes that it is easier to change the account number rather than return it to you for correction. He also has insight information that within the next year or two a new system will be in place; he thinks you can learn the account numbers at that time.

> In the meantime, you never know the errors that you are continually making.

The following points are extremely important.

> A new system in and of itself, will not correct the issue. Even if the current process is manual, a <u>correct</u> process should be in place to help ease the pain of learning a complete new system. It's much easier to incorporate a good process (even though it's manual) into a better process.
>
> One of the biggest mistakes organizations make is to put off process improvement because they want to wait for a new system.
>
> It's important not to automate a process or involve new software until you document and then remove waste from the current process.
>
> An ineffective process remains ineffective despite new technology, until the existing process has been optimized. [1]

What has this kaizen accomplished so far?

CCI's A/P kaizen team has done a lot in 3.5 days:

- Documented reality
- Identified waste in the current process
- Developed an ideal state
- Used "brainstorming" to generate ideas for improving the process (going from the current process to the future state process)
- Ranked the ideas using a Benefit/Effort matrix (A1 to B2)
- Rapid experiments – tested some of the new ideas and interviewed other departments involved in the new process

Under Jane Holmes' leadership, the team has also has learned a lot about how to do kaizen effectively. And, they've discovered areas where they can make immediate improvements.

But they are not done yet.

Modifying standard work

Once the rapid experiments are complete and process changes are tested, adjusted, and are working, you can generally begin writing or revising standard work.

In CCI's case, we have no standard work issues to resolve during the week. By agreement of the team, changes to standard work will wait until the 3-way auto-match is in place.

But we must not let standard work issues fall off the radar screen.

We will add them to the completion plan, with a date realistically placed in the future.

---

[1] Sometimes called "perfuming the pig." B. Maskell, S. Lilly, *Life's Little Lean Accounting Instruction Book; 365 Days of Self Help for Lean-Thinking Accountants*, (Cherry Hill, NJ, 2006) instruction # 46.

Note: If the 3-way auto-match is expected to take longer than 90 days, Crumple Crunch should write up standard work for the interim process. We recall Kim will be matching packing slip quantities against invoice quantities where we match from the receiving report.

If this change to Kim's process goes on beyond 90 days, it should be considered an "intermediate state" and A/P standard work should be revised. In this way standard work documentation is kept up to date and in pace with what is actually happening in the office.

Writing the completion plan

At this point in the kaizen, it's time to make sure all the unfinished "to do's" on the benefit/effort matrix are added to the 90-day completion plan.

The team reviewed the list and added details about what is being done, who is responsible, who is helping, when the project will be done, and its current status.

The CCI A/P kaizen team's completion plan looked like Figure 20.

R.I. Events	Projects	Do-Its	Description	Who	Resource	Completion Date	Comments	Status
			Schedule Kaizen event for Buyers standard work	John C.	Kathy A	15-Apr		
			Develop a price list for all purchased parts	Purchasing Mgr	John C	15-May		
			Set tolerance levels in place	John C.	Purchasing Mgr	1-Aug		
			Write Standard work for the new 3 way auto match process	Kim	Kathy A	15-May		
			Begin new auto 3-way match process	Kim	Kathy A	20-May		

Figure 20 CCI A/P Kaizen Completion Plan

Confirmed state

Because of the simplicity of this CCI's kaizen event, the team will be able to put the ideal state in place once the projects on the completion plan are finished. This is a function of the scope of CCI's kaizen event.

In many instances, completing a kaizen event will land you somewhere between the current and ideal state. This would be a function of the scope of any given kaizen.

We would call this the "confirmed state." Whatever the confirmed state is, it needs to be documented.

For example, if the CCI kaizen team judged they could not begin using the system 3-way auto-match within the next 90 days, but were confident they could use the receiving report indefinitely for matching, the confirmed state would be as follows:

The team reduced the cycle time by 15% (6.75 minutes to 5.75 minutes) using a receiving report to match to the invoice quantities instead of using manual purchase order & packing slip.

CCI would be aware they had not reached their ultimate target condition.

A3 review

CCI is just about done!

Jane knows the team needs to go back and review the A3 objectives. The objectives for this event are listed below:

1. Eliminate manual matching in A/P and move to auto-match using current software.
2. Remove waste & non-value added steps
3. Write standard work for new process

Jane asks the team if the objectives were accomplished. If not, why not? Is there still time to address the issues? If yes, now is the time. If not, decide what next step is appropriate and add to the "completion plan".

The team also has to finish the A3. If you remember, on the 1st day of our kaizen event, our A3 was only partially completed with the 1st three boxes. Initially Jane filled in the following:

Reason the event was chosen
Initial State
Target Conditions.

Now it's time to complete our A3 by filling out the last six boxes:

Current State
Ideal State
Benefit/Effort Matrix
Rapid Experiments
Confirmed State (Note: the "confirmed" state is also the "ideal" state in this instance.)
Completion Plan

The final A3 for CCI's A/P Kaizen is shown in Figure 21.

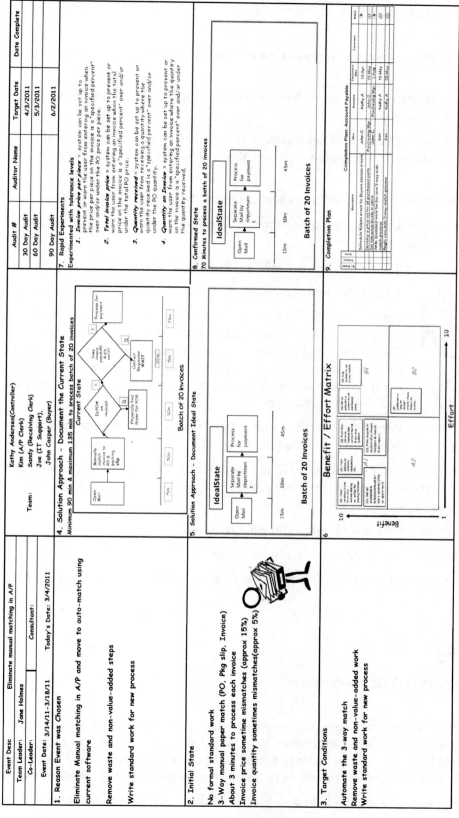

Figure 21 CCI's Final A3

Prepare the team's report out

At this point a kaizen team should be toward the end of day four, and ready to prepare its kaizen report for management.

Generally, presentations are given on Friday morning, but each company is different and may want to generate their own schedule.

Sometimes companies will wait until several kaizen events are complete and present them all at once at a scheduled time. There are also instances where there is no formal presentation, just a report to management.

Each company has their own format for preparing a report to management and/or a final presentation.

Some are more specific and require a specific format, while others are not so particular. The format is not as important as the content.

Remember, you are telling a story from beginning to end.

It's not all about the results, but also about how you arrived at the final results.

For example, CCI's kaizen team decided to use the A3 as an element in their final presentation. They used PowerPoint® and created one slide for each A3 box. Then they added pictures and other details to tell the entire story of who participated on the team, how their kaizen went along, the methods they used, a run-down of any rapid experiments and process changes they accomplished, and their completion plan.

Keep in mind, this is a simplified version. Adding graphics and additional slides is completely acceptable.

The CCI team, for example, showed a copy of the memo they sent to vendors and the results of their time observations and process changes that resulted in a 15% improvement in the time it takes to process vendor invoices.

Whatever it takes to tell the story is what you want to include.

I only caution that you are not too wordy, but hit on the main topics.

You want to keep your audience's attention and ensure continued management support!

Day 5

Report out to management

All team members and key managers, decision makers, and any other stake holders should be in the room. The audience can be as cross-functional as you want to make it. In CCI's case, they decided to invite key people from Operations, Purchasing and IT, because their support will be crucial in the future and their work will be impacted by changes to how A/P is handled. Key CCI managers were included.

In addition to the kaizen team, the following people were present to hear the team's report:

Steve Stark, CEO

Anne Johnson, CFO
Stacy Stiletto, Purchasing Manager
Morrie Harris, Operations Manager
Steve Timour, Buyer
Robbie Gunner, Lean Coordinator
Jim Jension, Value Stream Manager Electronics Packaging
Sarah Jones, Value Stream Manger Food Packaging
Pat Smith, Value Stream Manager Other Packaging
Sue Kraft, Receiving Manager
The entire Accounting Department

Post-kaizen follow-up

Ok, so you are finished with the kaizen event, but there are still projects on the completion plan.

Don't let the completion plan fall off the radar screen.

Remember, this is not the lean "Olympics!" You don't just have a week of meetings, do a final presentation, take all your bows, then on Monday go back to doing the same thing you did before the kaizen event.

"Kaizen" means continuous improvement. It's the event team's responsibility to make the improvements stick. This means being vigilant and finishing the completion plan.

Having weekly follow-up meetings with all team members will help people stay engaged and stave off complacency.

Not only do team members have an obligation to finish the completion plan but everyone needs to SUSTAIN THE RESULTS!

From experience, this is where companies often fail.

Don't be one of those companies.

How do we know our improvements are working?

There are standard tools you can use to stay on top of the changes that are happening. Don't fall into the trap of thinking this is no big deal. Our CCI example kaizen event has focused on a small kaizen.

Keep in mind the team is learning not just how fix A/P, but also but also how to kaizen. Part of being successful at kaizen is mastering change management tools and staying on top of many changes that might be happing at one time.

Red dot board

One sure way to know if your improvements are working is to implement what we call a "red dot" board.

Red dot boards provide a visual way to manage the incidence and frequency of issues that continue to crop up.

For CCI, after the completion plan was finished, Kim the A/P clerk, was still having issues with some areas of her work. The A/P kaizen team became aware of this during one of their regularly-scheduled follow-up meetings.

The team decided Kim needed to keep a red dot board for a while. This would show the team exactly what was happening, so they could figure out how to fix it. The team rightly viewed this as a sustainability issue.

How the red dot board works

There are several variations to a red dot board. The one the CCI team used (see Figure 22) simply states the types of issues in the column on the left, and the days of the week across the top. Then each time an occurrence of that particular issue happens, Kim put red dot under that day's occurrence.

Typically, the red dot board is kept in plain view of anyone walking past the A/P desk. Managers walking by can easily see what types of issues are frequently occurring.

In this case, on Monday there were 8 times when the price on the PO did not match the price on the invoice. Managers can decide if the issue is happening frequently enough to warrant getting to the root cause of the issue.

Sometimes it's helpful to count the dots and calculate the percent of the time that an issue occurs compared to the total # of invoices processed. In this case, Kim processed 251 invoices, and encountered a total of 15 problems, which yields a problem rate of 15/251, or about 6% (rounded) of the time.

Accounts Payable							
Red Dot - Issues	# of invoices processed	Weeks	Monday	Tuesday	Wednesday	Thursday	Friday
Price on PO doesn't match Price on Invoice	251		●●●● ●●●●				
Qty received doesn't match qty on Invoice			●				
Missing Packing List			●●				
Price descrepancies not received in time to take discount			● ●●				
Invoice Received late							
No PO # on invoice			●				

Figure 22 CCI's A/P Red Dot Board

Another tip: You can also use a red dot board for several weeks BEFORE the event to document the frequency and types of issues occurring. This pre-kaizen activity will help when documenting the current state map. The team will have solid data of the types of waste and frequency of occurrences in the process.

Going forward

Congratulations! You are now a trained A/P kaizen expert!

Get ready! Kaizen has a way of catching on.

Most likely, your organization will get to a point where prioritizing events becomes necessary due to the large number of requests.

The best way to prioritize events is to align them with company goals and objectives. You can also review the Diagnostic repeatedly, as your company makes progress on its lean journey. What kaizens you do, what issues you attack, and even what "perfection" looks like will of course vary according to your company's goals.

Your achieved progress gives you a new starting point each time.

For example, if one of your company goals is "to centralize accounts payable," then it makes sense to schedule kaizen events focused on accounts payable, such as the one we've seen CCI do.

This doesn't mean no other office kaizen events get scheduled. Such events should fit into a lower priority on the "future kaizens" list, if they make sense.

It's best to use a "kaizen request form" that any people requesting a kaizen event should submit. The form's layout is insignificant as long as it lists the event, a description of the problem it is supposed to solve, and has a way of prioritizing the event, such as how often and where it happens, any known ramifications of it (maybe something like "discounts are lost" or "customers hold up payment.")

This type of information can help management decide which events provide the most "bang for your buck" – or said differently, "the highest rate of return".

NOTE: In the beginning stages of kaizen it may not be possible to quantify monetary savings. It's difficult to put a dollar value on intangible improvements such as "reduce the time it takes for fill out an expense report". If each person filling out an expense report spends 30 minutes a week, and those completing expense reports are exempt salary employees, monetary savings are difficult to quantify.

In such cases, it's better to look for non-financial ways to measure improvement. There are many potential benefits for freeing up time and resources.

Here's a list of benefits that might flow from saving 30 minutes a week:

Cycle Time: Freeing up 30 minutes a week allows employees to use that time for value-added activities or lean training.

Wait Time: Reducing the time to fill out an expense report usually requires some simplification of the form. If we assume the form is written in a computerized format complete with drop down boxes for types of expenses, departments, and clear instructions, we can then assume the new expense report will reduce the amount of errors by eliminating such things like: invalid account numbers or departments. This will automatically decrease the wait time due to less expense reports being sent back to the user for corrections.

Training: By attaching specific standard work, the user is less likely to make a mistake.

Automation: Even a simple Excel spreadsheet can lessen the number of errors that may happen using a manual process.

Rework: Better controls = less rework.

Standard Work: Standard Work directs users to follow a set of instructions. Remember: you cannot hold users accountable for their actions if there is no standard work.

Visual Controls: One type of visual control is a "red dot board" which was reviewed earlier. In this instance, you can record additional issues that either are still happening pre-kaizen and new issues that have risen post-kaizen.

Standardization: It is obvious that standardization will reduce cycle time and rework, as well as simplifying the training process.

Creating a purchase order with fewer transactions: a buyers' kaizen for improving purchasing activities – another how-to example

This kaizen event will be much more complicated than accounts payable because at CCI there are two buyers and each has two different processes: one for MRP and the other for supermarkets.

Since we have the A/P kaizen under our belt, it seems appropriate to move to an event with more detail to give you an understanding of different scenarios.

Going back to the A/P kaizen, you'll remember there was a follow up on the completion plan that stated: "Schedule Kaizen Event for Buyers Standard Work". CCI's management team has concluded that this should be the next office kaizen event.

Jane Holmes will again lead the event.

Some background

The buyers at CCI have been extremely busy over the last several months. With this whole lean implementation going on in Operations, they have been learning about supermarkets and have actually set up supermarkets with two of their preferred suppliers.

All other raw materials are still using the traditional MRP method.

The buyers (John and Steve) are being tossed around in many directions. At this point they feel their jobs are harder because, while changes are being made on the production floor, the familiar traditional transaction-based system for creating a purchase order is still in place.

Keeping up with the transactions is taking a toll on their time, causing plenty of overtime to keep up with demand.

Fortunately, management has agreed to allow both of the company buyers to participate in this event. Management is completely on board with lean and understands the importance this event contributes to lean success. Each buyer has a backup person doing their job during kaizen week.

Who's cooking up change?

Let's see how CCI's kaizen team tackles the buyer's challenge.

The kaizen team will be following the step-by-step "recipe" for successful kaizen we saw applied to A/P. It worked well. CCI is more experienced now. We'll narrate here the steps they follow.

In case you need to, please refer to The Team Leaders Guide section of this book.

Picking the best team

Jane has chosen the following team, including herself as the kaizen leader:

John Casper, Buyer. John understands the importance of having the correct price on the purchase order, but because he is very busy it's extremely difficult to ensure perfection on his part.

Stacy Stiletto, Purchasing Manager. Stacy sets up supplier agreements and has authority to make changes that affect supplier agreements and anything else involving purchasing.

Steve Timour, another Buyer for a different value stream. Steve is fairly new to Crumple Crunch and finds his job difficult to keep up with because he's just now learning about supermarkets and also having to use MRP.

Robby Gunner, Lean Coordinator. Robby works in the lean office and has been through some extensive training setting up supermarkets and has also worked for other lean companies.

Kathy Andersen (the Controller) has the authority to authorize changes that affect accounting and control, thus she has direct connections with the auditors in the event auditor approvals are necessary.

James (a receiving supervisor) who has been instrumental in helping set up supermarkets.

Suzie (forklift driver) who is excited about the new lean implementation and also works with the supermarkets daily bringing materials in and out.

Preparing the A3

Jane has conducted interviews with the participants, observed the current process, and has prepared the following A3 to lay out the issues and scope of the Buyer's kaizen. The Buyer's kaizen is an extension of the A/P kaizen, and at the completion of this event Jane believes the company will move from the "traditional" area on the Diagnostic to the "developing a framework" for the Accounts Payable and Procurement Process.

Jane reviews the Diagnostic and creates the A3. See figures 23 and 24.

Category & Goal	Traditional	Developing a Framework	Managing by Value Stream	Lean Business Management
Accounts Payable & Procurement Shift from high volume and procedurally complex processes to minimum transactions with built in controls	Each order of materials and supplies is documented with a regular purchase order. All materials and supplies received are checked and documented. **We perform a manual 3-way match to ensure the accuracy of invoices prior to entering into system.**	We have made great strides in simplifying accounts payable. We now use the system to 3-way match. We have issued blanket purchase orders for high moving material, and have started to identify and certify strategic suppliers. Systems are now in place to prepare for "pay on receipt" of materials for key suppliers.	Most of our key suppliers deliver material based on kanban cards. Suppliers deliver frequently (daily or twice weekly) and are set up to "pay on receipt", eliminating the need for an invoice. For slow moving or one time material purchases, we use the system to 3-way match.	Materials are paid on receipt when the products are shipped. All payments are electronic and there is no AP process.
	Kaizens for Next Stage	**Kaizens for Next Stage**	**Kaizens for Next Stage**	
	Credit Cards for Small Purchases Blanket POs for Large Purchases Certify Strategic Suppliers **3-way match on computer**	Eliminate three-way match Voucher for payment on receipt	Electronic payment for all suppliers Expense materials when received	
Your "Score"				
Now (Current State)	2			
6 Months From Now		2		
18 Months From Now				

Figure 23 Review of CCI's Diagnostic Results

Event Desc	To Create Purchase Orders with less Transactions		Team:	John (Buyer), Stacy (Purchasing Mgr), Steve (Buyer), Kathy (Controller), James (Receiving Supervisor), Suzie (forklift driver), Robby (Lean Coordinator)		Audit #	Auditor Name	Target Date	Date Complete
Team Leader:	Jane Holmes					30 Day Audit		8/4/2011	
Co-Leader:		Consultant:				60 Day Audit		9/3/2011	
Event Date: 7/11/11 to 7/15/11	Today's Date: 7/5/2011					90 Day Audit		10/3/2011	
1. Reason Improvement was Chosen Reduce transactions to allow buyers to free up time to focus on developing supermarkets and managing those already set up.									
2. Initial state About 3 hours / day is focused on transactions for creating purchase orders. Each purchased part requires a new purchase order every time it is ordered. Each of the two buyers processes about 250 purchase orders per month for raw material. Buyers are working overtime because they are trying to implement and manage supermarkets as well as do their normal job.									
3. Target conditions Reduce the time it takes to create a purchase order by reducing transactions. Remove waste / non value-added work Write standard work for the new process.									

Figure 24 Buyer's Kaizen A3

Day 1

The team starts with introductions and also spends a good portion of the morning in training. Jane knows there are people present who are not familiar with the approach the team will use.

If necessary, thoroughly review how to use an A3, the kaizen steps shown in Figure 2 in the Team Leader's Guide.

Jane knows continuous improvement will become a way of life at CCI; she wants to establish a baseline of knowledge about how to go about kaizen.

Document the current state

After the morning break the team begins the process of documenting the current state.

Because we have two buyers in this event, we will document each buyer's current state separately.

This is important. It's too easy for one buyer to just agree they perform the same steps as another. If each process is documented separately, you will most likely see a substantial difference. Also, we will start with Steve because he is fairly new to Crumple Crunch and less knowledgeable of the process. If we start with John, it's likely Steve may just agree to John's process because he may not want to admit he does something in his process that may seem non-value added.

Since Steve says his process is different for creating a purchase order for a non-supermarket process versus those that are now in a supermarket, both processes will be documented separately. The four processes to be documented are listed below:

1. Steve's non-supermarket process
2. Steve's supermarket process
3. John's non-supermarket process
4. John's supermarket process

Let's start with Steve's non-supermarket process.

Document current state (Steve) – Non-supermarket process

Jane asks Steve to walk the team through the steps of creating a purchase order. Suzie has agreed to scribe. She will use yellow Post-its® for the non-supermarket process versus blue Post-it® for the supermarket process.

Using a different color helps visually distinguish the non-supermarket from the supermarket process for everybody, but especially for people not present for the kaizen event, yet interested in seeing the process.

Steve's non-supermarket process:

Steve starts by saying he runs the MRP report first thing in the morning. Next, he has the cycle counter go into the warehouse and check stock for some of the items MRP is telling him to order.

Jane asks Steve how he knows which items to count.

He says there was a time when he had the cycle counter check everything, but she wasn't finishing the counts before he was required to place the orders. As a result, he now has her count only critical items, usually those that are high dollar or higher quantity items. He also noted that management is now looking at inventory turns and questioning why certain items have a high dollar value in inventory.

Steve is now more careful not to order more than required. In the past he would frequently order 10% to 20% more than MRP required to ensure he would have enough to fulfill his orders, plus a buffer.

Once Steve's inventory checks are complete and adjusted in the system, usually a couple of hours after he runs the report, Steve re-runs the MRP report to account for the changes in inventory.

Steve is finally ready to create a purchase order.

He enters all the required information, supplier number, item #, quantity, etc. He lets the system default to the last price paid as the price that will be listed on the purchase order.

Steve scans and emails the purchase order to the supplier. Many times the supplier changes the price on the purchase order and sends it back to Steve to correct on his end. In every case, he agrees with the supplier and corrects the price in Crumple Crunch system, then scans and e-mails the corrected purchase order back to the supplier.

Kathy asks Steve why he depends on the supplier to give him the correct price. Being in accounting and finding many mistakes, Kathy is skeptical about taking the word of the supplier.

Steve answers, "I rarely have accounts payable come back to me with incorrect pricing because the supplier most always invoices us for the price they told me to input on the purchase order. The only time the price changes is if I changed the quantity later, which might fall into a different price tier, or if I order the item so far in advance that the price changes before the item is received. Both of those instances are rare, of course."

Note: Steve and John have only recently begun correcting prices on the PO in the system as a result of the A/P event back in March. In the past, they were hand writing the correct price once they received it from either the Purchasing Manager or the supplier, which caused the A/P clerk to camp out at their desk every Monday morning because the prices on the PO in the system often did not match the invoice. In fact, there are still times this happens, but it's a lot less frequent.

Kathy doesn't look pleased with that answer, but before Kathy can respond, Jane notices Kathy's facial expression and says "We understand this is what you do today in your current state. Let's move on."

Steve is finished with the purchase order once he receives an e-mail confirmation from the supplier.

Steve says he then just waits for the order to arrive based on the scheduled delivery date.

The rest of Steve's job revolves around phone calls made because of back orders, late orders, wrong item delivered, etc. He also has to account for high levels of inventory, go to daily meetings, and a variety of other duties.

Jane agrees there are many other parts to the buyer's role, but the scope of the kaizen is centered on purchase orders. Remember... stay within your defined scope because addressing other issues will likely cause you to not finish the intended scope, resulting in zero accomplishment.

Figure 25 represents the current state map the team prepared for Steve's non-supermarket process.

Notice how the team had to extract the main steps in the process from Steve's narrative.

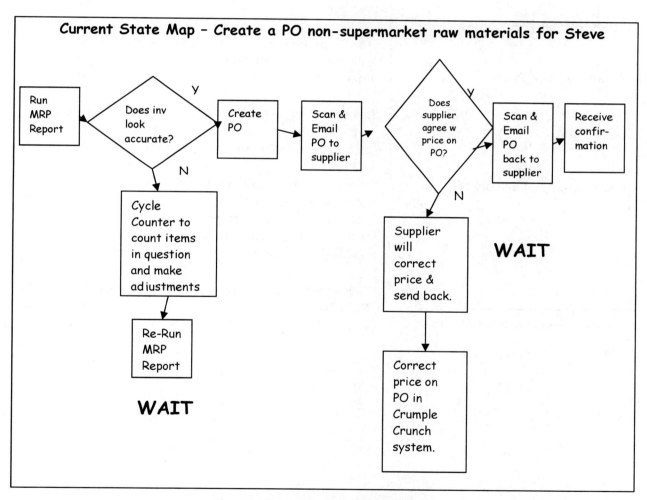

Figure 25 Steve's Non-Supermarket Process

Document current state (Steve) – supermarket process
Next the team examines Steve's current state process for creating purchase orders for the two suppliers set up on supermarkets.

First, Steve explains that each morning he goes to the supermarket and collects all the kanban cards that are at the kanban posts. These cards represent what's been used in the supermarket and require a reorder.

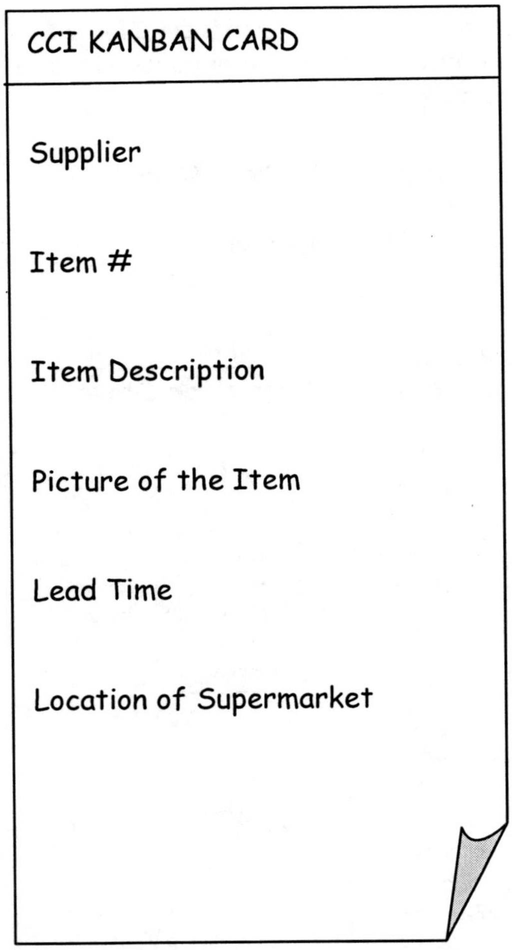

```
CCI KANBAN CARD

Supplier

Item #

Item Description

Picture of the Item

Lead Time

Location of Supermarket
```

Figure 26 Format of CCI's Kanban Cards

Once Steve gathers the cards he groups them for like items and then creates a Purchase order for each item. The creation of the purchase order is the same as the process used when ordering for a non-supermarket process.

Steve does not check inventory or have a cycle counter verify it because the system is set up so that kanban cards are not generated until the product is used. He "automatically" knows they need the items. Inventory is visually managed by the plant.

Steve does, however, go through the same process for allowing the supplier to change the price on the purchase order as he does with the non-supermarket process.

Steve scans and e-mails the purchase orders to the supplier.

Once a confirmation is received….that's it.

Steve's process is easier for those items in supermarkets because he doesn't have to deal with cycle counts. It is not, however, easier for creating the purchase order. The creation of the purchase order is still transaction oriented and filled with opportunities for improvement.

When complete, the Steve's current state map looks like the Figure 26.

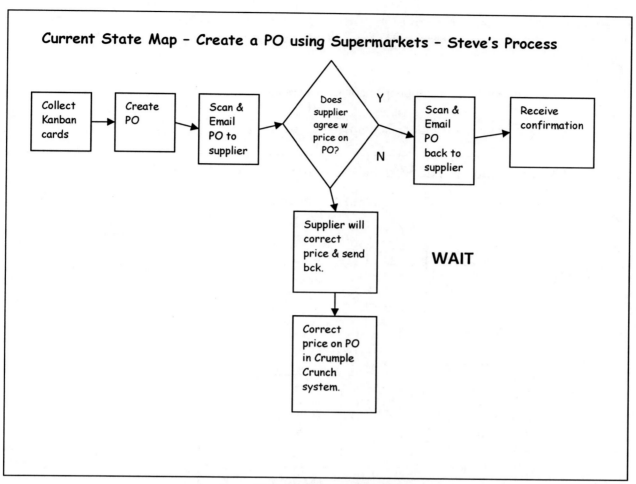

Figure 27 Steve's Supermarket Process

Document current state (John) – non-supermarket process

John's current state mirrors Steve's non-supermarket process except for one area where the system creates the purchase order. John contacts the purchasing manager to make sure the price is correct for those items where he's unsure, while Steve relies on the supplier to correct the price.

Some members of the team are curious as to why the price would be incorrect, while others believe that is a double check point.

Both John and Steve explain the reasons, listed below:

1. Some items have tiered pricing, which means the price paid depends on the quantity ordered. Typically, the more ordered the cheaper the price. The system does not account for tiered pricing.

2. The item is new and there is no cost information in the system.

3. The price has not been updated since the last price change.

Jane asks if a different step is performed for each reason listed above. In each instance, John explains that he emails the Purchasing Manager for those in question (some he knows are correct based on his experience.)

As you recall, Steve relies on the supplier to correct the price.

Figure 28 represents John's current non-supermarket process.

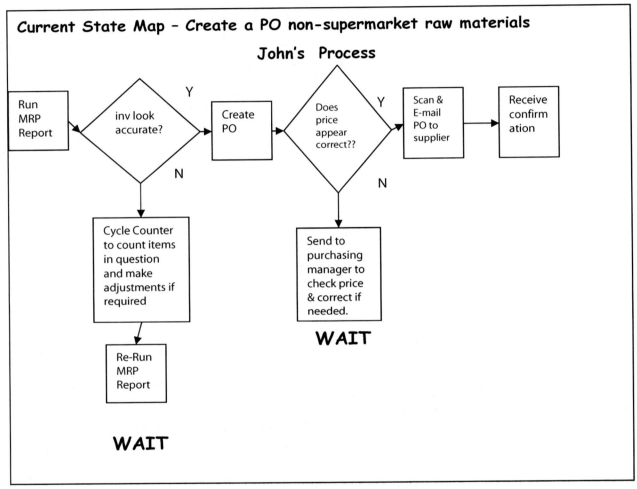

Figure 28 John's non-supermarket Process

Document Current State (John) – Supermarket Process

John's supermarket process is the same as Steve's except John checks the price (as he does in his non-supermarket process) before sending the purchase order to the supplier.

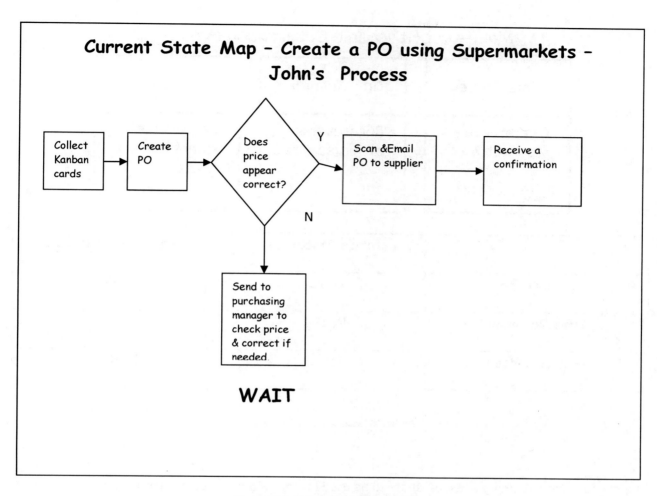

Figure 29 John's Supermarket Process

Time observations

Once the current state is documented for all four processes, the team is ready to do time observations.

Remember the makeup of the observation group from the Team Leaders Guide.

In this case, the team splits up into two groups, one for Steve's processes and one for John's processes. Each group includes 3 team members, as shown in Figure 30.

Make-up of the Time Observation Group

Time Keeper	Time Recorder	Map Recorder
• Operates the stop watch	• Records the observed times	• Creates the standard work sheet

	John's Processes	Steve's Processes
Time Keeper	Jane	Suzie
Time Recorder	Robby	Stacy
Map Recorder	James	Kathy

Figure 30 Observation Group Roles

Before the event, IT set up a test database to be used for the kaizen. In reality, neither Steve nor John could possibly perform 10 separate time observations in one day because they do not process enough purchase orders.

> As the culture begins to change as a result of doing lean, more people are willing to help in areas not part of their daily responsibilities.

The completed time Observation sheets for both Steve's and John's Non-Supermarket process are shown in Figures 31 and 32.

Time Observation Sheet

Project Area / Machine: Steve - non supermarket

Date:

Batch of 10 Purchase orders

NO.	Component Task	1	2	3	4	5	6	7	8	9	10	Component Task time	Points Observed
1	Run MRP Report	310 / 310	300 / 300	305 / 305	310 / 310	310 / 310	310 / 310	308 / 308	310 / 310	310 / 310	310 / 310	308	
2	Contact cycle counter to count inaccuracies	120 / 430	0 / 300	0 / 305	120 / 430	121 / 431	0 / 310	130 / 438	0 / 310	77 / 387	0 / 310	57	The time is zero if the buyer believes the inventory is accurate
3	WAIT for counts	7260 / 7690	0 / 300	0 / 305	7280 / 7710	7210 / 7641	0 / 310	5200 / 5638	0 / 310	8010 / 8397	0 / 310	3496	The time is zero if the buyer believes the inventory is accurate
4	Create Purchase Orders	1810 / 9500	1720 / 2020	1800 / 2105	1800 / 9510	1805 / 9446	1800 / 2110	1750 / 7388	1690 / 2000	1700 / 10097	1805 / 2115	1768	Time varies depending on how many items are on a purchase order
5	Scan & Email Purchase Orders	360 / 9860	300 / 2320	300 / 2405	320 / 9830	360 / 9806	360 / 2470	330 / 7718	320 / 2320	360 / 10457	300 / 2415	331	
6	WAIT for Supplier to send back puchase order confirmation	3200 / 13060	3200 / 5520	3200 / 5605	3200 / 13030	3200 / 13006	3200 / 5670	3200 / 10918	3200 / 5520	3200 / 13657	3200 / 5615	3200	In time observation, team could not wait for supplier to send back 10 batches,
7	Review Purchase orders from supplier to see if the prices were changed	200 / 13260	180 / 5700	180 / 5785	199 / 13229	197 / 13203	199 / 5869	201 / 11119	187 / 5707	195 / 13852	196 / 5811	193	
8	If price was changed, go back into system & change price	0 / 13260	120 / 5820	102 / 5887	130 / 13359	0 / 13203	0 / 5869	0 / 11119	0 / 5707	150 / 14002	0 / 5811	50	
9	If price changed, scan & Email corrected copy back to supplier	0 / 13260	300 / 6120	297 / 6184	290 / 13649	0 / 13203	0 / 5869	0 / 11119	0 / 5707	298 / 14300	0 / 5811	119	
10	Receive confirmation & save in email folder	60 / 13320	52 / 6172	62 / 6246	61 / 13710	60 / 13263	53 / 5922	57 / 11176	59 / 5766	62 / 14362	68 / 5879	59	
	TIME FOR 1 CYCLE in minutes	222	103	104	229	221	99	186	96	239	98	160	In Minutes

Figure 31 Steve's Non-Supermarket Times

Time Observation Sheet

Project Area / Machine: John – non supermarket **Date:**

Batch of 10 Purchase orders

NO.	Component Task	1	2	3	4	5	6	7	8	9	10	Component Task time	Points Observed
1	Run MRP Report	305 / 305	305 / 305	310 / 310	306 / 306	305 / 305	303 / 303	310 / 310	310 / 310	310 / 310	308 / 308	307	
2	Contact cycle counter to count inaccuracies	120 / 425	0 / 305	121 / 431	0 / 306	0 / 305	0 / 303	0 / 310	130 / 440	0 / 310	0 / 308	37	The time is zero if the buyer believes the inventory is accurate
3	WAIT for counts	5800 / 6225	0 / 305	7200 / 7631	0 / 306	0 / 305	0 / 303	0 / 310	6521 / 6961	0 / 310	0 / 308	1952	The time is zero if the buyer believes the inventory is accurate
4	Create Purchase Orders	1650 / 7875	1710 / 2015	1690 / 9321	1595 / 1901	1701 / 2006	1702 / 2005	1653 / 1963	1680 / 8641	1595 / 1905	1660 / 1968	1664	Time varies depending on how many items are on a purchase order
5	If price doesn't appear correct, send to purchasing mgr WAIT	210 / 8085	0 / 2015	0 / 9321	0 / 1901	0 / 2006	0 / 2005	60 / 2023	256 / 8897	0 / 1905	0 / 1968	53	In time observation, team could not wait for supplier to send back 10 batches,
6	Scan and e-mail purchase order to supplier	310 / 8395	310 / 2325	312 / 9633	315 / 2216	308 / 2314	310 / 2315	318 / 2341	330 / 9227	321 / 2226	308 / 2276	314	
7	Receive confirmation & save in email folder	60 / 8455	60 / 2385	62 / 9695	58 / 2274	58 / 2372	58 / 2373	59 / 2400	61 / 9288	57 / 2283	56 / 2332	59	
8													
9													
10													
	TIME FOR 1 CYCLE in minutes	141	40	162	38	40	40	40	155	38	39	**73** In Minutes	

Figure 32 John's non-supermarket times

Some things to notice

In order to get 10 consecutive counts, James (the receiving supervisor) was able to pull several different people from receiving to do cycle counts that day to speed the process. If not for that help, it wouldn't have been possible to count the items in question all in one day.

> Not every type of event requires 10 time observations. It really depends on how important "time" is to the event. This event is particularly sensitive to time because the buyers are working overtime to finish their daily tasks. If, for example, the wait time was the majority of the issue, timing the processing steps 10 times may not be worth the effort.
>
> **THINK "Benefit versus Effort"**

Also note that the wait time for the cycle counter is an average of 10 time observations even though there were no stock counts needed for in many of the time observations.

Remember, the buyers only have the cycle counter check items in question, which may not happen every day. The average truly represents the average time for cycle counting over a long period of time to account for those times there is no need to count.

Also, the cycle time in Steve's process (no. 6) "WAIT for supplier to send back confirmation" ranges anywhere from 30 minutes to an hour. The team used 3200 seconds for all 10 time observations. This is probably a good average and since this is a step we have an opportunity to eliminate, it's not worth wasting time doing 10 separate batches and wait 10 different times.

Map Recorder: Creating the standard work sheet (spaghetti diagram)

As instructed in the leaders guide, use a relevant floor plan diagram to create the 'standard work sheet.'

Kathy volunteers to draw (record) the travel distance for each step performed away from the immediate work area for Steve's process and James volunteers for John.

This step is performed simultaneously with the time observation.

Because there was no map of the area already drawn, Kathy used a piece of paper and hand drew desks, people, receiving area, supermarket area, etc. She makes a copy and uses one copy for Steve's spaghetti diagram and James uses the other for John's spaghetti diagram.

Once finished, Kathy and James combine the spaghetti diagrams for both Steve and John for non-supermarket items into one drawing. Steve's diagram is on the left of the map while John's is on the right.

We created our example using the computer, but doing a hand-drawn sketch is preferred.

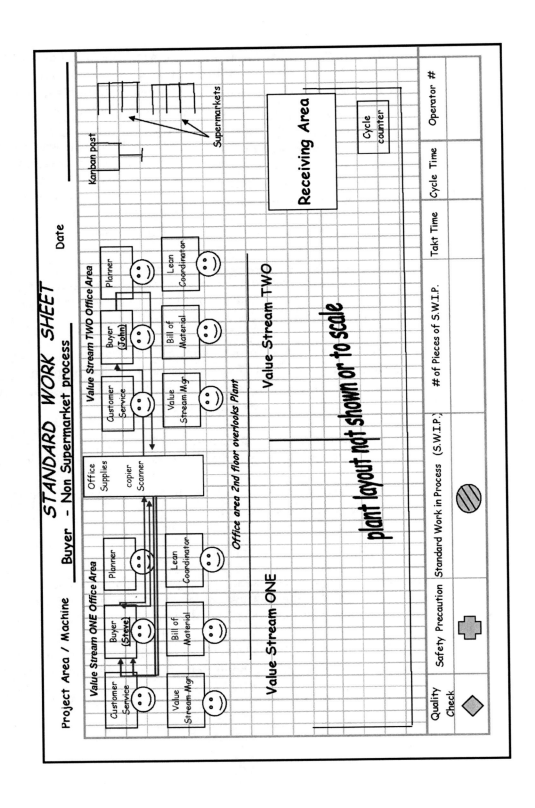

Figure 33 Results of Non-supermarket Travel Observations

As you can see, Steve's travel is solely to the scanner and back to his desk. All other steps are completed at his desk. John doesn't travel to the scanner as often as Steve.

Creating the time line

Next, based on actual observations, the team prepares a time line and adds it to the bottom of the current state map for both Steve and John's non-supermarket processes.

We've written processing time below the line and wait time above.

The batch size of 10 is labeled on the current state map.

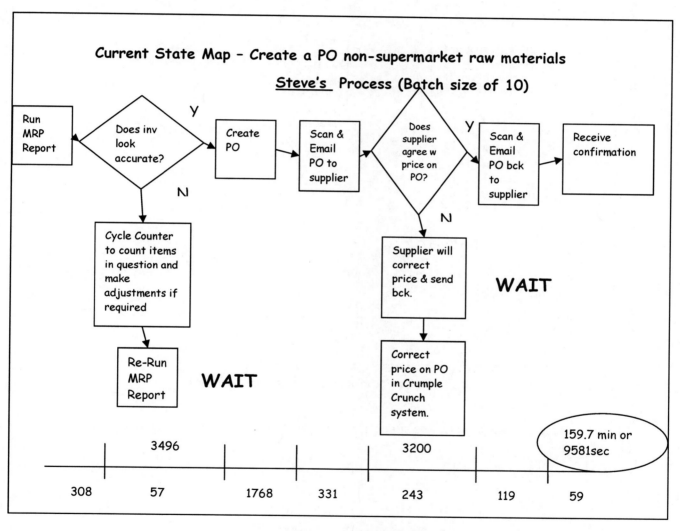

Figure 34 Steve's Current State with time line

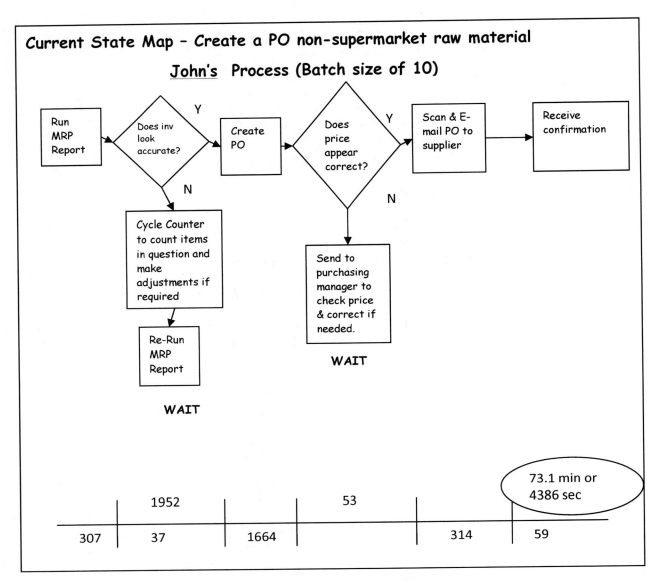

Figure 35 John's Current State with Time Line

The same process is repeated for the supermarket items. Figures 36 and 37 show these time observations.

Time Observation Sheet

Project Area / Machine: Steve - supermarket
Date:

Batch of 10 Purchase orders

NO.	Component Task	1	2	3	4	5	6	7	8	9	10	Component Task time	Points Observed
1	Collect Kanban cards	482	480	485	481	482	492	480	481	491	499	485	
		482	480	485	481	482	492	480	481	491	499		
2	Create Purchase Orders	1649 1590	1750	1720	1762	1725	1724	1690	1700	1620	1693	Time varies depending on how many items are on a purchase order
		2131 2070	2235	2201	2244	2217	2204	2171	2191	2119		
3	Scan & Email Purchase Orders	351	325	310	310	350	310	311	322	327	310	323	
		2482 2395	2545	2511	2594	2527	2515	2493	2518	2429		
4	WAIT for Supplier to send back puchase order confirmation	3200 3200	3200	3200	3200	3200	3200	3200	3200	3200	3200	In time observation, team could not wait for supplier to send back 10
		5682 5595	5745	5711	5794	5727	5715	5693	5718	5629		
5	Review Purchase orders from supplier to see if the prices were changed	201	200	185	201	195	194	200	185	196	186	194	
		5883 5795	5930	5912	5989	5921	5915	5878	5914	5815		
6	If price was changed, go back into system & change price	117	0	0	0	125	0	0	0	0	0	24	In time observation, team could not wait for supplier to send back 10
		6000 5795	5930	5912	6114	5921	5915	5878	5914	5815		
7	If price changed, scan & Email corrected copy back to supplier	297	0	0	0	290	0	0	0	0	0	59	
		6297 5795	5930	5912	6404	5921	5915	5878	5914	5815		
8	Receive confirmation & save in email folder	61	53	61	60	60	60	58	59	61	67	60	
		6358 5848	5991	5972	6464	5981	5973	5937	5975	5882		
9													
10													
	TIME FOR 1 CYCLE in minutes	106	97	100	100	108	100	100	99	100	98	**101** In Minutes	

Figure 36 Steve Supermarket Time Observations

Time Observation Sheet

Project Area / Machine: John - supermarket
Date:

NO.	Component Task	Batch of 10 Purchase orders										Component Task time	Points Observed
		1	2	3	4	5	6	7	8	9	10		
1	Collect Kanban cards	482	480	485	481	482	492	480	481	491	499	485	Time varies depending on how many items are on a purchase order
		482	480	485	481	482	492	480	481	491	499		
2	Create Purchase Orders	1649	1590	1750	1720	1762	1725	1724	1690	1700	1620	1693	
		2131	2070	2235	2201	2244	2217	2204	2171	2191	2119		
3	If price doesn't appear correct, send to purchasing mgr WAIT	250					175	0		0	145	114	
		2381	2070	2235	2201	2244	2392	2204	2171	2191	2264		
		325	325	310	310	326	327	311	325	327	311		
4	Scan & Email Purchase Orders	2706	2395	2545	2511	2570	2719	2515	2496	2518	2575	320	
		61	53	61	60	60	60	58	59	61	67		
5	Receive confirmation & save in email folder	2767	2448	2606	2571	2630	2779	2573	2555	2579	2642	60	
6													
7													
8													
9													
10													
	TIME FOR 1 CYCLE in minutes	46	41	43	43	44	46	43	43	43	44	**44**	In Minutes

Figure 37 John's Supermarket Time Observations

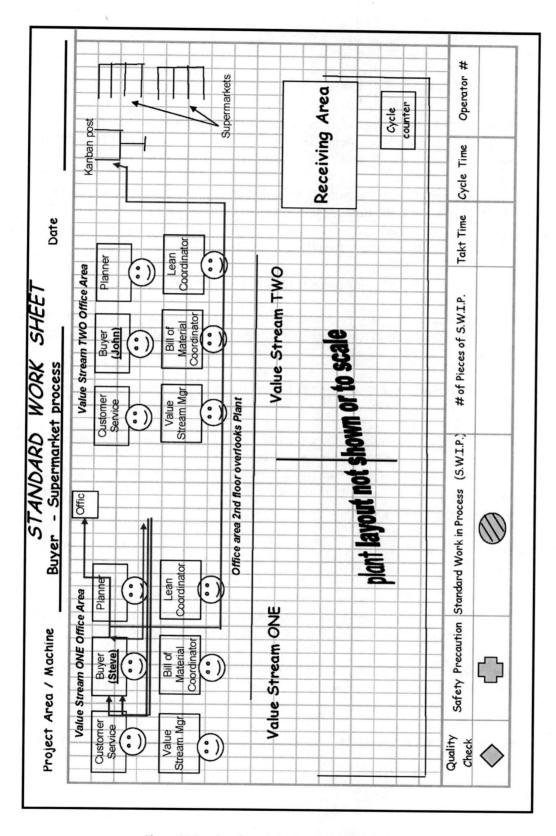

Figure 38 Results of Supermarket Travel Observations

Time observation results

The results of the time observation were eye-opening for the team.

So what do the results mean?

First off, they found out their initial ideas about processing cycle time were not far off from the estimate of about 3 hours/day on the A3, but it's hard to tell the exact amount of time with so many non-value added steps in the process that vary greatly from day to day.

Plus, depending on whether the PO's are non-supermarket or supermarket also makes a difference. Looking at the time observations, the non-supermarket process for creating a purchase order is over double the time for the supermarket process. However, because the supermarket items are ordered in smaller quantities, they are ordered more frequently.

Kathy immediately asks why all purchased parts are not in a supermarket?

Robby answers by saying that the 2 year plan is to put about 80% of purchased parts in supermarkets, but there will always be about 20% that will not be in a supermarket either because they are slow moving or one-time purchases.

The team also noticed that John's non-supermarket cycle time is considerably less than Steve's, 160 minutes for a batch of 10 versus 73 minutes.

The main differences are that John requests fewer cycle counts. Because of John's longevity with the company, he relies on his tribal knowledge of knowing what items have a higher frequency of being wrong, and he also knows what items are high dollar without having to look anything up in the system. He can basically tell in an instant what he thinks is wrong and requires a cycle count. Supermarkets do not require a cycle count!

John is also a bit faster processing purchase orders; again he knows the screens in the computer system like the back of his hand.

Moreover, John checks the price before he sends the purchase order to the supplier. The purchasing manager is fairly quick responding to John's requests, while Steve sends the purchase order to the supplier first and has to wait for them to confirm. The supplier typically has a slower response time.

In a supermarket environment, however, John rarely needs to check the prices since the items are high moving and typically the same items are ordered on a weekly basis, thus the buyers are more likely to intuitively know if the price is correct.

All in all there appears to be a lot of waste in the process, particularly in the non-supermarket process.

Day 2

Because they were documenting a more complicated process, the team ended up cutting into day two when documenting reality and time observations, finishing just before 1st break. This is a good example of why some flexibility in the schedule is desirable.

As a team progresses, they may discover a process is more complex than they anticipated. The schedule should have enough "give" to accommodate this.

Master chefs seem to know intuitively that a given recipe might need adjustments; they naturally apply their experience, a little more salt, a tad more pepper, in order to achieve the best result.

Document the ideal state – non-supermarket raw material process

Now that we're finished our time observations of the current state, we're ready to begin documenting the ideal state.

Like the current state, the team will document the ideal state for the non-supermarket process separately from the supermarket process, except since this is the ideal state, both Steve and John's process will be the same, thus there is no need to document the ideal state separately between buyers. (It may not be obvious to you, but our end result will be new standard work ... hence, both buyers' processes will be the same.)

Jane reinforces to the team that the ideal state is what <u>should</u> happen and this is not the time to figure out <u>how</u> it should happen. "All we're doing right now is documenting an "ideal" state," she said. See the team leader's guide for instructions for the ideal state.

The team begins by agreeing an MRP report will still be used to determine requirements.

Robby explains to the team that in an ideal "lean" state we would use what's called a "heijunka box" to level load uneven demand, and also serve as a pull trigger to order those raw materials that are not in a supermarket – mainly slow-moving or new items. It's similar to a schedule in that it prioritizes production of orders and can also when signal to order a purchased part that is not included in the kanban system.

The team is not familiar with the term "heijunka box." It's hard for the team to grasp the concept with such a brief explanation. Nonetheless, because Robby is understood to be a lean expert, they agree to keep it in the ideal state because they believe it may not be something we can do right now anyhow.

Next there is a team consensus that the buyer should not have to review inventory accuracy because the only items that will not be in a supermarket are new items (hence, no inventory), or slow-moving items (which CCI will not keep any inventory), thus this step is removed.

There will still be purchase orders for items that are not in a supermarket. A formal document is needed as a contract between the supplier and Crumble Crunch. The system should be able to automatically route the purchase order to the supplier, eliminating the e-mail step.

So the team came up with the following ideal state for non-supermarket raw materials. See Figure 39 below.

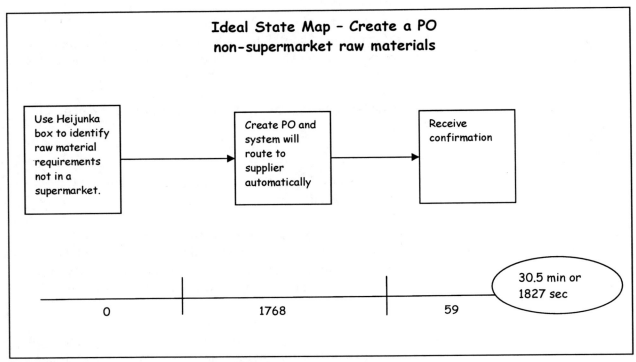

Figure 39 Ideal State - Non-supermarket Purchases

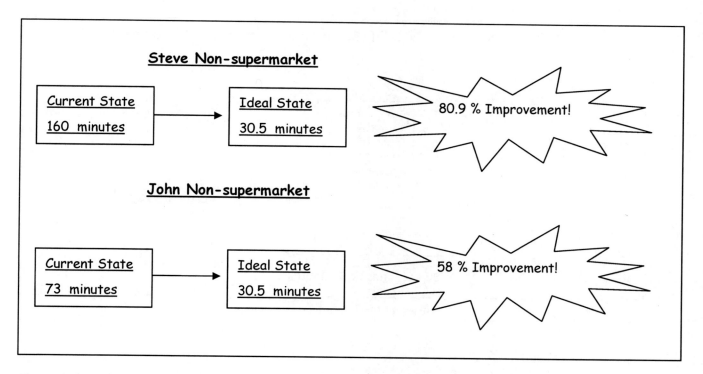

The cycle time for the heijunka box is assumed to be zero because the team makes the assumption that IT would automate a report to show demand for non-supermarket items, similar to an automated MRP report, or some may prefer the term "automated heijuka".

Creating a PO and receiving confirmation used the same cycle time as in the current state. It's important that you do not come up with a different cycle time for the parts of the process that didn't change because then you will not be comparing apples to apples.

And because Steve had a different cycle time for the same processes as John, the team had to decide which to use. They decided to use Steve's cycle time because it was their consensus that not everyone was as quick as John.

Note: There may be instances when the faster time is used. For example, if the slower cycle time is due to a person who doesn't normally do that part of the process, or if that person is exceptionally slow for whatever reason.

Document ideal state— supermarket raw material process

The team decided in the ideal state the kanban cards can be scanned and automatically routed to the supplier. In fact, this may be the task of someone on the plant floor. At this point, it's not important who does the actually scanning.

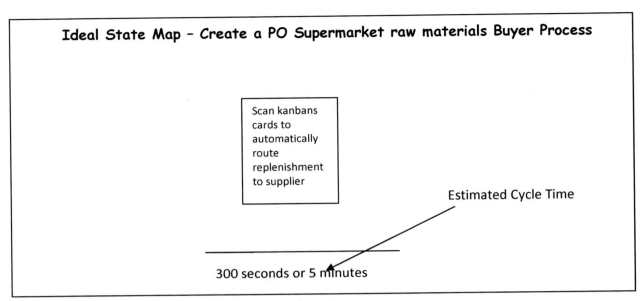

Figure 40 Ideal State Supermarket Items

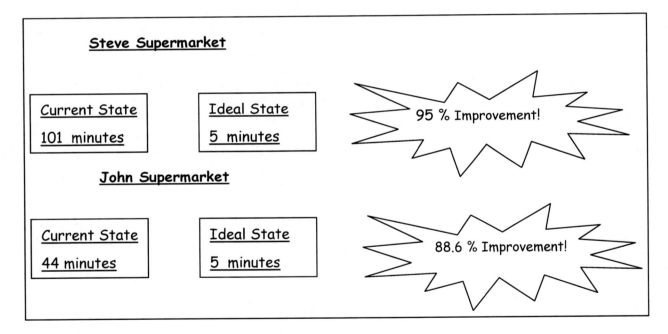

Wow! Look at the possibilities of improvement: 95% improvement for Steve and 88.6% improvement for John.   This was big news.

The team was finished with the ideal state by lunch time. They planned to start the brainstorm session after lunch.

Brainstorm session – non-supermarket raw material process

As instructed in the team leader's guide, this is an exercise that is done individually. Each person is instructed to come up with at least one, but preferably two or more ideas for each of the areas of waste. In other words, the areas of the "current state" that were removed from the "ideal state". The team is trying to figure out how can we get from "where we are" to "where we want to be?"

The leader is responsible ahead of time for developing a list of questions that, if answered, will lead the team to the ideal state. It is extremely important that the questions are carefully thought out because if the questions are not all inclusive, the current process cannot possibly reach its ideal state goal. The leader writes these questions on a large Post-it® easel pad.

The areas of the current state that were removed from the ideal state are marked "WASTE" as outlined below in Steve's non-supermarket process.

Be sure to point out the areas of waste to the team. Even though it may seem obvious to the leader, it's not always obvious to the team. In most cases, the person doing the job believes what "lean" considers to be "waste" (also known as "muda") may seem like a normal part of their job. [1]

The same rule applies for Steve's supermarket process and John's non-supermarket and supermarket processes. Let's review the non-supermarket process.

---

[1] Note: Taken in the light of value to the customer, most of what accounting does can be called "muda." Even so, it's necessary to running the company and keeping robust business controls in place. So we should consider it necessary waste.

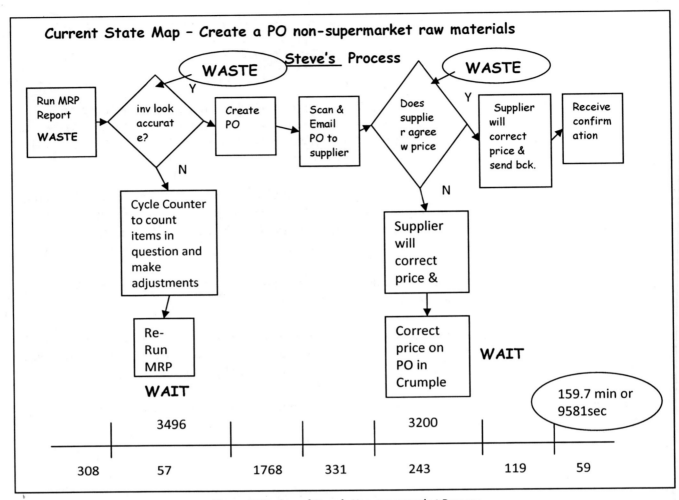

Figure 41 Review of Steve's Non-supermarket Process

Jane prepared the following questions for the team to answer that will move the process from its current state to the ideal state for both supermarket and non-supermarket processes.

Remember, while the questions are designed so that by brainstorming each questions will bring you from your current state to your ideal state, it doesn't necessarily mean we will be at our ideal state at the end of this event.

Our goal is to help the team understand that regardless of whether or not we meet our ideal state this week, we want to strive to be there someday.

If we don't have an understanding of where we want to eventually be, we will never get there because we think the improvements we've made this week are the best we can do. While it is the best we can do today, there is still opportunity for improvement. The team will keep thinking about reaching that ideal state long after the event, and will someday accomplish that goal.

Jane's questions for the **non-supermarket** process:

1. How do we move away from relying on MRP reports?

2. How do we move away from relying on the supplier or purchasing manager to give the buyer the correct price?

3. How do we avoid cycle counts for non-supermarket items?

4. How do we eliminate scanning purchase orders before sending to the supplier?

5. How do we implement a heijunka box?

Additional questions for the **supermarket** process that were not covered above:

1. The kanban cards are not visible to the buyers causing excessive walking time. What's an alternative method?

2. How do we implement a scanning method for kanban cards?

3. Can we avoid creating a purchase order for every order since the kanban card is now the trigger to replenish? What's an alternative method?

Refer to the Team Leader's Guide for brainstorming instructions. This is a vital step in the improvement process. If this step is not completed properly, the outcome will not be optimal. The kaizen may not accomplish what has been planned.

When the team finished with their ideas, Jane gathered the Post-it® notes and arranged them on a Post-it® easel pad as displayed on Figure 42.

Jane was careful to only post the idea ONE time if there were duplications of the same idea.

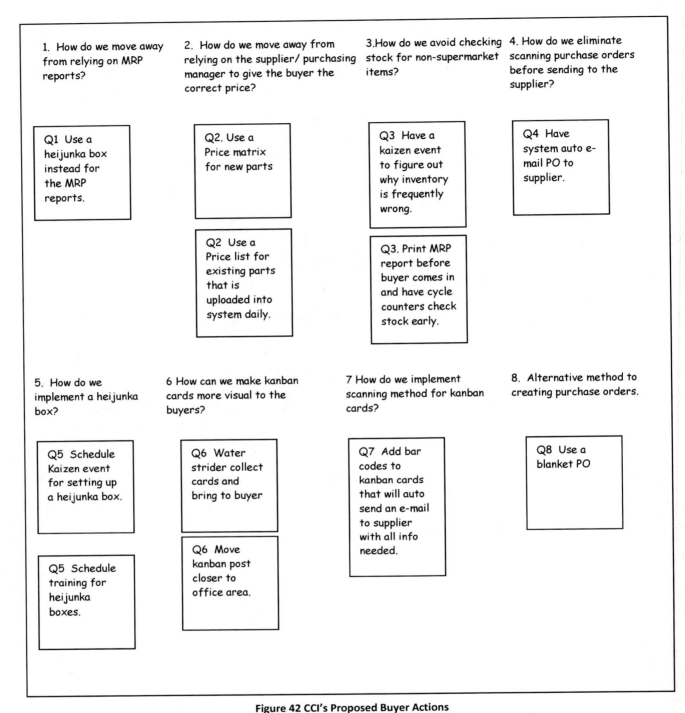

Figure 42 CCI's Proposed Buyer Actions

Benefit/Effort matrix

Now that all the brainstormed ideas are displayed, Jane helps the team rate their ideas using a "Benefit/Effort matrix". Again, refer to the Team Leaders' Guide for instructions about how to put together the matrix.

> During a company's lean journey, it's important that each dept/area does not move faster or slower than another. For example, if supplier agreements are made to eliminate tiered pricing for small runs, but not communicated to the buyers, this could potentially cause buyers to continue ordering larger quantities.
>
> **An excellent chef learns to get the entire meal on the table at the same time.**

A blank Benefit/Effort matrix is shown in Figure 43 below:

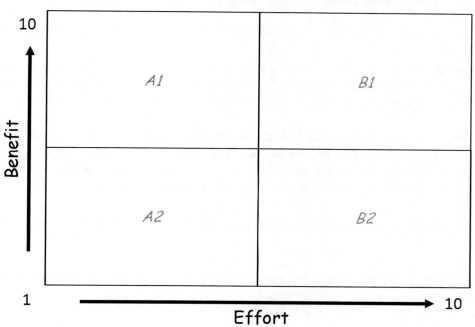

Figure 43 Blank Benefit / Effort Matrix

With Jane in the lead, the team begins to consider each proposed action, beginning with Question # 1 How do we move away from relying on MRP reports?

1st brainstorming idea:

> Q1 Use a heijunka box instead for the MRP reports.

Robby explains to the team that a heijunka box is a way of level loading uneven demand.

91

It's similar to a schedule because it prioritizes production of orders and can also signal to order a purchased part that is not part of the kanban system.

Robby doesn't feel Crumple Crunch is ready for using a heijunka box, especially not to the degree that it signals to order purchased parts. There's a lot that has to happen before Crumple Crunch can tackle heijunka boxes.

Robby adds, "It's imperative that CCI doesn't get ahead of ourselves on our lean journey or we could end up missing orders, late orders, or other negative impact on the customer. Let's consider this a **B2** for this event because we can still accomplish what's on our A3 without implementing heijunka boxes just yet. "

Jane wholeheartedly agrees with Robby. She noticed the look on everyone's face when the word "Heijunka" was used earlier. It was obvious most of the team never heard of a heijunka box. In fact, one team member said "heijunka box" sounds like a controlled substance!

Jane had brought a short video with her that explained heijunka boxes and showed it to the team.

After the video and a few questions, the team agreed to make this idea a **B2**, meaning the effort to implement is extremely difficult and while the benefit is very important to the success of "lean" in general, it's not part of the scope of this event, nor does it hinder the success of this event.

Be cautious here! A heijunka box is something that can be implemented in the later stages of lean. For this team though, it's very important to stick to the scope of the event. While a heijunka box is definitely part of the Ideal state, and we want the team to be aware of its existence, we do not want to put something in our 90 day completion plan that will not happen in 90 days

Jane takes this Post-it®from the easel pad and attaches it to the proper area on the Benefit/Cost matrix. In this case **B2**.

Question #2 – How do we move away from relying on the supplier/ purchasing manager to give the buyer the correct price?

1st brainstorming idea:

> Q2. Use a Price matrix for new parts

This idea was a combination of many that were basically saying to use some kind of price agreement that lists all the possible combinations of a purchased part. Formally, this is called a "price matrix".

Stacy, the Purchasing Manager already has a price matrix for all preferred suppliers that she can easily share with the buyers. In fact, this is what she uses when the buyers call for a price of a new part.

After about 1 hour of training, she can pass along the matrix to the buyers and they no longer need to call her or wait for the supplier to give them a price for a <u>new</u> part. This price matrix will cover all possible combinations of purchased parts from each of our preferred suppliers.

Stacy agrees to train the buyers this week, thus this idea becomes an **A1**.

Question #2 — How do we move away from relying on the supplier/ Purchasing Manager to give the buyer the correct price?

    2nd brainstorming idea:

> Q2 Use a Price list for existing parts that is uploaded into system daily.

As with the price matrix, Stacy also keeps a price list in a spreadsheet for all <u>existing</u> purchased parts. This list contains the supplier name, supplier #, part #, current price and the unit of measure. Stacy can share this spreadsheet with the buyers, but it would benefit everyone if it could automatically upload into the computer system so that the correct price for what's being ordered will default in the purchase order screen.

Stacy agrees to meet with IT to see if it's an option to automatically upload the spreadsheet nightly, but she's not sure if it's something IT can whip up this week, nor is she certain it's even a possibility.

Jane thinks we should make this idea an **A1** for now. We can move it later if necessary.

Question #3 – How do we avoid checking stock for non-supermarket items?

    1st brainstorming idea:

> Q3 Have a kaizen event to figure out why inventory is frequently wrong.

Without question, the team agrees that an event is necessary to figure out why inventory is frequently wrong. This is not something that can be accomplished this week. The scheduling of the event will go on the completion plan. This idea belongs in quadrant **B1**.

    2nd brainstorming idea:

> Q3. Print MRP report before buyer comes in and have cycle counter check stock early.

Both Steve and John like this idea, but Robby points out that this idea is putting a Band-Aid® on the problem and not getting to the root cause, which is why the issues are occurring in the first place.

Jane steps in and agrees with Robby, but she also points out that this may be a temporary fix until the inventory accuracy kaizen event takes place.

"Although we will schedule that event to happen within the next three months, some of the results may not happen immediately after our current event." Also, as Jane points out, if this idea turns out to be an easy thing to do, we should look into it.

This idea is obviously an **A1** because if it doesn't work we will know this week.

Question #4 – How do we eliminate scanning purchase orders before sending to the supplier?

    1st brainstorming idea:

> Q4 Have system auto e-mail PO to supplier.

Since there is not an IT person on this event, the team will have to meet with IT sometime during the kaizen week to see if this is possible. The team believes this should be an **A1**.

Question #5 – How do we implement a heijunka box?

    1st brainstorming idea:

> Q5 Schedule Kaizen event for setting up a heijunka box.

    2nd brainstorming idea :

> Q5 Schedule training for heijunka boxes.

Robby quickly reminds the team that they already decided heijunka boxes were out of the scope of this event back in question #1. The team agrees, thus making this idea a **B2.**

Question #6– How can we make kanban cards more visual to the buyers?

    1st brainstorming idea:

> Q7 Water strider collect cards and bring to buyer

    2nd brainstorming idea:

> Q7 Move kanban post closer to office area.

Jane reminds the team that most of the travel distance in the spaghetti diagram was from walking back and forth to the kanban post to pick up kanban cards. She poses the question: Could the Kanban post be moved closer to the office area; or perhaps, move the buyers closer to the kanban post?

John is opposed to making a change in this area even though it's a lot of walking on the buyers' part. He believes that at this stage in their lean journey, it is important that he visit the kanban area regularly to visually see if the kanban levels are set properly and to observe the activity.

Because this is all new to him (and also to Steve) he feels the need to have visibility to the area even though this requires more walking.

The team agrees with John. Jane also agrees. This idea is listed as a **B2**; essentially it will not be done at this time.

Note: As lean progresses, the buyer's role becomes that of a "demand analyst" who analyzes changes in demand, where as now the role is more of a clerical position since the majority of the work is pushing paperwork through the process. In a traditional buyer role, there is little time to analyze or get to the root cause of issues. Lean changes all that!

Question #7 - How do we implement a scanning method for kanban cards?

    1st brainstorming idea:

> Q8 Add bar codes to kanban cards that will auto send an e-mail to supplier with all info needed.

Adding bar codes to the kanban cards is definitely something that should be done in the early stages of lean because waiting will only make it that much more difficult as more kanbans are put in place.

The team is unsure of the time it will take to do this, plus there are many other areas affected.

They are sure this will take longer than this week, but also know it's important to saving time and transactions. The team decides this idea is rated **B1** and it will be added to the completion plan as a meeting to decide next steps.

Question #8 – Method to avoid creating a PO for every order?

1st brainstorming idea:

Q8 Use a blanket PO

Stacy, the purchasing manager is not sure how using a blanket purchase order will help.

She's been taught that a purchase order is required for every item. Kathy is in agreement. Robby, on the other hand, has some ideas and will work with them during the rapid experiment time of the event. The team agrees and this idea becomes an **A1.**

The next figure shows the team's completed Benefit / Effort Matrix.

CCI's completed Benefit / Effort matrix

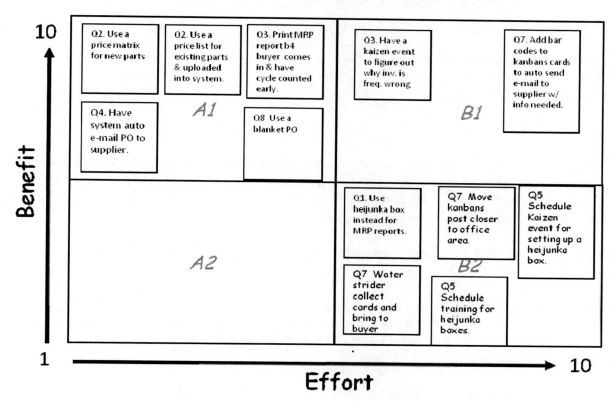

Figure 44 CCI's Completed Benefit / Effort Matrix

The team barely finished the brainstorm session on day two. In fact, they stayed an extra half hour to finish. Everyone was anxious to finish and didn't mind staying.

 Day 3

Doing rapid experiments

If you recall from the team leader's guide, this is the part of the kaizen where the team can finally begin working on some of their ideas. This is commonly called "rapid experiments" because the team is experimenting with their ideas within the time constraints of the kaizen.

Also, remember to bring a camera along to take before and after pictures of the improvements you're about to make! This will make it easier tell your story when it comes time to report to management.

Jane and the team review the matrix (in Figure 44) before they develop a plan of action for their rapid experiments.

Jane knows that the bulk of the work is in the A1 quadrant, meaning these ideas could potentially be accomplished during the kaizen week. Jane realizes that all the work in the A1 quadrant requires input from the buyers, thus it doesn't seem feasible to break up the team into smaller groups to work on ideas simultaneously. It also doesn't appear the team is behind schedule, giving an even stronger reason to work on the A1's as a group.

Beginning with the first idea in A1….

```
Q2. Use a
price matrix
for new parts
```

As Stacy stated earlier, she has a price matrix for all preferred suppliers for new purchased parts, thus after about 1 hour of training, she can pass along the matrix to the buyers and they no longer need to call her or wait for the supplier to give them a price for a new part. This price matrix will cover any purchased part from any of our preferred suppliers.

Stacy gathered the price matrixes for each preferred supplier, which ended up to be 12 different types of matrixes.

Stacy began training the team (particularly the buyers) how to use each matrix. After about 15 minutes, Robby suggested the team write standard work for each process because they are all different. Moreover, the standard work can be used as a training document for new buyers or for training backups.

The process of training and writing the standard work took the majority of the morning on day 3.

Note: There are times during an event where there isn't time to complete the standard work. While it's okay to move Standard Work to the completion plan, it's worth the time to begin writing the standard work during the event because it is sometimes harder than it looks, especially for people not good with software like spread sheets and word processing. This will give the person responsible for writing the standard work some practice and also time to ask questions. People have a tendency to avoid completing something they are not familiar with.

Also, standard work is best developed by the people who just redesigned the process and combining their thinking. Plus, while they are writing Standard Work they often find gaps in their thinking which they might otherwise have missed.

Below is a sample of the Standard Work the team created.

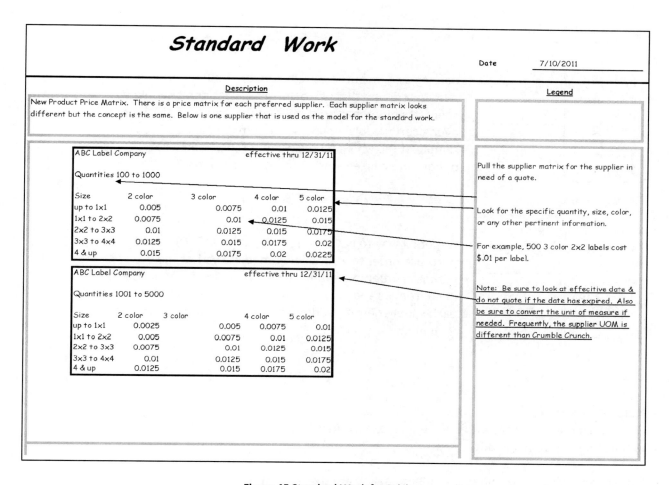

Figure 45 Standard Work for Pricing

Once this was complete, Jane removed the Post-it® for this idea from the Benefit/Effort matrix.

While the team had worked on the price matrix, Jane used her time to set up a meeting with IT to meet with the team just after lunch. Jane knew IT would need to be involved in many of the ideas in **A1**.

Jane and the team prepared a list of questions for IT. Looking at the ideas below, the team decided to ask IT the following questions:

Note: Jane knows from experience that IT is generally willing to help, but this requires the kaizen team be very specific with their requests and not ambiguous in any way. Doing this makes it more likely that IT will respond quickly with less guesswork and definitely less rework.

Questions for IT the team developed
2nd idea in A1....

Q2. Use a price list for existing parts & uploaded into system. → We currently have a spreadsheet file that houses our most recent prices for all purchased parts. The file contains the part #, description, current price per unit, and the supplier, each as a separate column. Is there a way to upload the spreadsheet file into our system so that when a purchase order is created, the price will populate the "price" field in the create purchase order screen? (Give IT a printed copy of the PO screen with the field highlighted and also a copy of the spreadsheet file) If yes, what information do you need from us to allow this to happen?

3rd idea in A1....

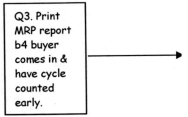

Can the system automatically run the MRP report at a designated time that will determine what items should be counted, thus generate a stock count report for all items over a certain dollar value or quantity on hand? (Give IT a sample of the MRP and cycle count report and what options are chosen when setting up to print)

4th idea in A1....

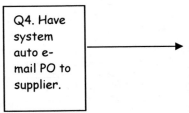

Is there a way to have the system automatically e-mail a purchase order to a supplier immediately after the purchase order is created? If yes, what information do you need from us and in what format? Obviously IT will need each supplier e-mail address and contact information at a minimum.

Meeting with IT

After lunch the team met with two people from IT, the IT Manager and another IT person who is more familiar with system uploads.

IT was very receptive to the team's ideas. Below are the responses from IT.

2nd idea in A1....

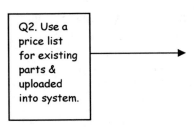

In order to upload a file from a spreadsheet to our current system, IT will need to look into the exact formatting required. They suggested we e-mail a copy of the spreadsheet, and they also took the hard copy of the PO screen. They will get back to our team by the end of the day today with an answer.

3rd idea in A1....

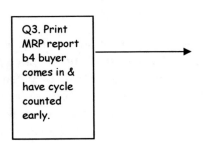

Yes, IT can certainly automatically run an MRP report for any specific time. They can also generate a stock count report for specific items. This is very easy and can be finished within a couple of hours once the team defines parameters, i.e. time of day to run report, dollar value, and quantity on hand.

4th idea in A1....

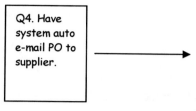

Yes, IT can easily set up the system to auto e-mail the purchase order to the supplier. In fact, the system has a built in function for e-mailing purchase orders, however, we are not using this function. IT walked the team through the system function and also printed the help screens. The team will need to add the supplier e-mail and contact information into the master supplier screens within the system before this function will work.

The team profusely thanked IT and said they would discuss the options and get back with them later that afternoon.

Continuing the rapid experiments

Once IT left, the team went back to each option individually and discussed each item again, this time getting together the information IT has requested.

Beginning with the 2nd idea in A1:

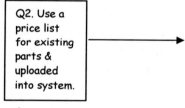

As IT suggested, Stacy e-mailed a copy of the spreadsheet file she used for preferred supplier current pricing. Beyond that, we have to wait for IT to come back with an answer.

3rd idea in A1....

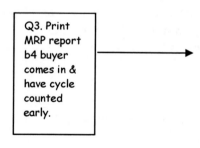

As suggested by IT, the team began to develop the parameters of the MRP & cycle count report. They came up with the following and provided this information to IT:

1. MRP report to run at 5AM each weekday.
2. Inventory valued at over $3000 or any quantity greater than 5000 will generate on the cycle count report.
3. MRP will generate again at 8am after cycle count adjustments have been made.

4th idea in A1....

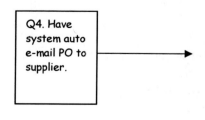

Both John and Steve provided a list of e-mail and contact information for all preferred suppliers. The team split up the list and began entering the information into the system. They were finished within 35 minutes.

Next, they tested the process with one supplier and it worked perfectly.

Yay! One more idea completed and removed from the brainstorming matrix.

We will, however, need to incorporate this new step into the standard work later.

5th idea in A1....

| Q5 Use a blanket PO |

As you recall, Stacy and Kathy were not sure how using a blanket purchase order will help lessen the transactions for creating purchase orders because the buyer would still have to go into the system and input the quantity being received, which is called a "release".

Robby, on the other hand, has some ideas from a company where he previously worked.

He explained that this company used a regular purchase order as a blanket. In other words, a regular purchase order was created for an unlimited quantity of a particular purchased part.

When the kanban card signaled a re-order, the same purchase order was used for that particular item EVERY time.

Receiving was easy because the packing slips always referred to the same purchase order, and because there was an unlimited quantity, there was never an issue, and a "release" was NEVER needed.

The buyer, however, would still have to notify the supplier of the order. Until the kanban cards are set up to scan and automatically e-mail to the supplier, the buyers can copy/scan and e-mail the kanban cards to the supplier as long as the purchase order number is on the copy of the kanban card being e-mailed to the supplier. This is a short term solution.

In the long term, however, CCI will need the bar codes on the kanban cards, so that when scanned with a bar code reader, will send all the required information to the supplier. For the bar code process to work with the supermarket process, it's not a waste of time to set up now, even though it may take extra time to copy and scan the cards before e-mailing these to the supplier.

This is a lot for the team to think about.

Jane directs the team, "Since we are close to the end of day 3, let's think about this and come back to it tomorrow morning, day 4."

Day 4

The team starts out the day with a review of yesterday's rapid experiments. Since this is the last day of the event, this is going to be a busy day.

They decide to plan their day by spending the majority of the morning wrapping up the rapid experiments and whatever is left will have to go on the completion plan. They will spend the afternoon preparing the completion plan, the confirmed state, the final A3, and the report to management.

Jane directed the team back to the "blanket PO" idea they were working on at the end of the day yesterday.

Robby and John had stayed late on Day 3 (without being asked) and together they came up with a demonstration of how the blanket purchase order idea would work in their system.

John explained to the team that a regular purchase order would be created for each part number currently in a supermarket. The quantity on the purchase order would be for the highest # the system will accept. This same purchase order will be used for one year, then a new one will be issued. If the price changes, the buyer has the ability to change the purchase order price.

Note: This approach cannot be used for non-supermarket purchased parts because many of those items have tiered pricing, meaning the price changes depending on the quantity ordered. This makes it difficult to manage. Moreover, there is no kanban card to provide the supplier for replenishment. A purchase order is still needed for every order as a signal to the supplier to re-order.

Supermarket purchased parts, on the other hand, have one price because they are high moving items and Stacy has already made agreements with the suppliers to purchase a specific amount for the entire year, but delivery of the parts should be only when a kanban card is generated signaling replenishment. Therefore, the price is fixed for a specific time period no matter what the quantity ordered each time.

Jane asks how long it will take to move all supermarket items on this system, train, and write standard work. Robby and Steve think it will be about 30 days because there are a lot of purchase orders to write, receiving must be trained, standard work written, etc. The team agrees to move this to the completion plan with a completion date of 30 days.

Jane also received the following information from IT that morning:

2nd idea in A1:

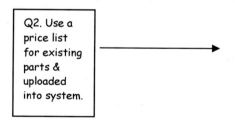

In order to upload a spreadsheet to our current system, an addon program will have to be purchased for $600 that allows the system to accept an upload from the spreadsheet into the purchasing module. There are some specific formatting requirements, but instructions will come with the software. CCI can also view a demo prior to purchasing.

The team is excited. They decide rather quickly that the $600 is worth spending on the new software addon, provided the demo works as promised. Robby notifies IT.

3rd idea in A1....

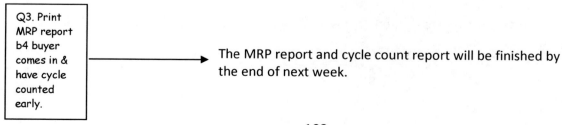

The MRP report and cycle count report will be finished by the end of next week.

Wrapping up rapid experiments

Before moving on, Jane asked the team to finish the rapid experiments and re-cap what's complete. With each rapid idea that is complete, be sure to mark "complete" on the Post-it® As you see in Figure 46.

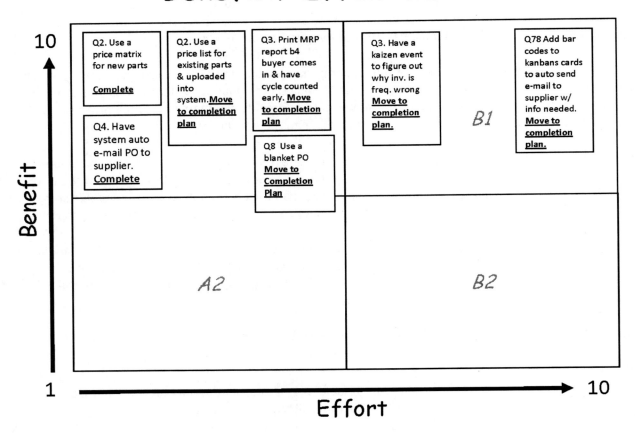

Figure 46 Revised Benefit / Effort Matrix

Standard work

Once the rapid experiments are complete, you can generally begin writing Standard Work.

In this case, the CCI buyers revised their Standard Work for any new processes put in place.

The kaizen team was able to finish the Standard Work for the buyers' price matrix; they will have to wait to complete or modify existing Standard Work for the changes made to the MRP and cycle count report and auto e-mailing the PO to the supplier.

When blanket purchase orders are created, that will also require new or modifications to existing Standard Work.

The Purchasing Manager will need to complete Standard Work for uploading the price list to the system and for modifying the spreadsheet.

It is difficult to write or modify Standard Work for a new process without actually testing the new processes for some period of time. In most cases, the process may work slightly different that you originally thought, plus in the instance of having new addon software, you do not have screen shots or all the information needed to write the Standard Work until the new process is actually in place.

For these reasons, CCI added Standard Work to the completion plan.

Completion plan

We've talked a lot about the completion plan throughout this book.

Now it's time to make sure all our unfinished "to do's" on the benefit/effort matrix are added to the completion plan.

Again, this is a team effort. It's important to have enough information to understand the "to do" when you look at it several days or weeks after the event, and the specifics have left your memory. Also make sure the "who" is always a person on your team. The resource can be outside the team, but that person must know the expectation. Give them a copy of the completion plan and keep them updated.

Figure 47 shows CCI's Completion Plan.

Completion Plan: Buyer Create Purchase order process					
Description	Who	Resource	Completion Date	Comments	Status
View demo for add on software for uploading excel files to system	Team	IT, John	15-Jul		⊕
Purchase software for uploading excel files to system.	IT, John	IT, John	16-Jul		⊕
Make necessary formatting changes to excel file once software is purchased and uploaded	IT, John	IT, John	30-Jul		⊕
IT to finish MRP & cycle count report	IT, John	IT, John	15-Jul		⊕
Set up new PO process complete with standard work.	Robby, John	Steve, Stacy	10-Aug		⊕
Set up meeting to decide the next steps needed to add bar codes to kanban cards.	Robby	Stacy	14-Aug		⊕
Set up a kaizen event to figure out why inventory is frequently wrong.	Stacy	Kathy	14-Aug		⊕

Figure 47 Buyers Kaizen Completion Plan

In the completion plan above, you'll notice the "to do" for <u>buying the new software to upload the price list</u> is broken down into three parts.

First, the team will view the demo software, purchase it, then make necessary changes to spreadsheet file formats.

This was broken out into three parts because it's easier to manage, plus it's in sequence to what has to happen and in what order. If, for example, it ends up the demo does not work as planned, and the software is not purchased, those "to do's" will be marked complete on the completion plan with a comment explaining why the software wasn't purchased.

Management should be made aware of this decision and the parties responsible will need to modify the Standard Work to account for not making this change. This is not an anticipated outcome and should be avoided if at all possible. Sometimes IT or management can think of a different solution. In any case, going back to how things were is usually not the answer.

Confirmed state

It's rare that a company will move from its current state to its ideal state with one kaizen event. Typically, you will end up somewhere between the current and ideal state which is called the "confirmed state".

This is exactly what happened with CCI's event. Here's the process the team used to arrive at the confirmed state.

They had a number of alternatives to evaluate.

The team went back to the current and ideal state, to see where CCI ended up.

First they looked at the non-supermarket process, comparing and combining elements from the current state and the ideal state.

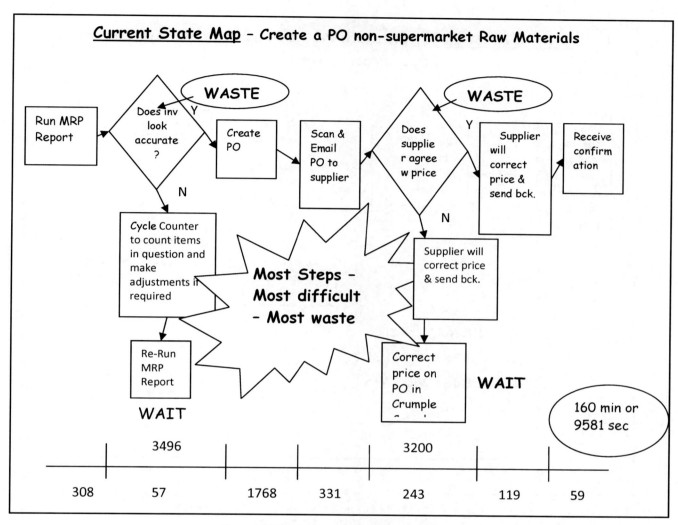

Figure 48 The Team Examined the Current State

They then looked at John's processes and devised a process that would work for both buyers.

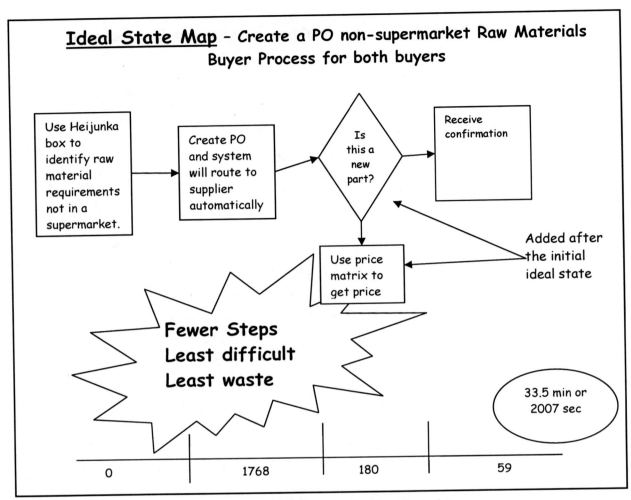

Figure 49 The Team Reexamines the Ideal State for Both Buyers

They were able to devise a confirmed state based on what the kaizen has accomplished. See Figure 50.

First off, notice only Steve's process is listed under the current state and not John's process. The team used Steve's cycle times from the time observations since his cycle time was longer. They made the assumption that not everyone is as quick as John.

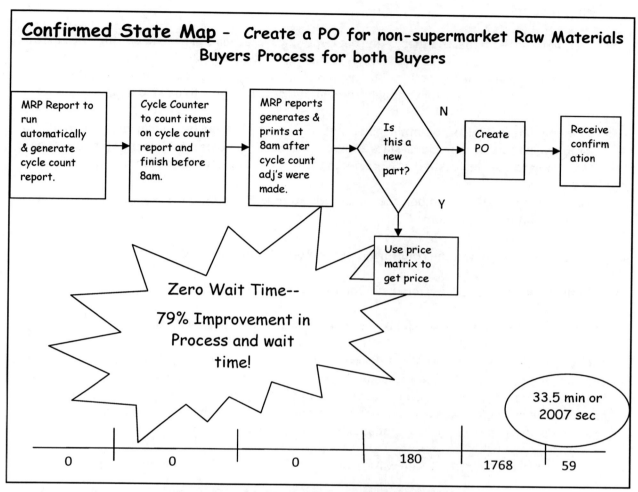

Figure 50 CCI's Confirmed State for Non-Supermarket Items

The team reviewed all their accomplishments this week as listed below:

    As you recall, the team decided an MRP report was needed, but the report will be set up to run automatically at 5am, generate a cycle count report, and then run again at 8am after the cycle count adjustments have been made. The cycle counts will take place before the buyer comes in so the wait time for the buyer is eliminated. Remember, we are only looking at the cycle time and wait time for the buyer since the buyer is the scope of this event, not the cycle counter.

    Since the price list is automatically uploaded into the system from the price list in excel, there is no need to check the price for existing items. For new items, however, the price will be listed on the price matrix. Not all items are new, so this step isn't performed each time.

    Purchase orders will still be created for non-supermarket items

    The buyer will no longer have to check with the purchasing manager or the supplier to check the purchase price. Remember, the buyer will now have a pricing matrix for new purchased parts and a price list for existing parts will be automatically uploaded to the system, thus no need to check pricing.

Just then the team realized that in the ideal state the buyer will still have to use the price matrix to get a price for new parts. This was not thought of in the initial ideal state because it was before the brainstorming session. The team was looking at what should happen and they weren't to a point where they thought through the details of how to make it happen.

It is common to think of something later that wasn't initially thought of in an ideal situation. No problem, just add it to the ideal state above. Keep in mind, however, 3 minutes (or 180 seconds) are added to the ideal state that were not in the original ideal state earlier in this manual.

No more scanning! Remember, the system will automatically route the purchase order to the supplier through the system.

So how does the team know if the confirmed state is more efficient than the current state?

Let's add the cycle times to the bottom based on the following information:

We know that the MRP report will take no time because it's run automatically.

The cycle counter will still take about the same amount of time as before. Although the wait time of 3496 (for the buyers) is eliminated, even though the time to count is still the same. What's changed is the sequence, allowing the buyer to avoid waiting for the cycle counter. It's done before he arrives in the morning. Keep in mind that we are only considering the buyer cycle time and by rearranging the sequence we have not added to the cycle counter time.

The MRP report generating at 8am will also involve zero time since it's runs automatically.

The team did a time observation to see how much time it would take to look up a new part on the price matrix. The average time was 3 minutes (180 seconds).

Creating a purchase order is 1768 seconds, same as in the current state.

Receiving confirmation is 59 seconds, same as in the current state.

Once the cycle times were added to the confirmed state the team is puzzled why the ideal state cycle time is the same as the confirmed state cycle time.

Suzie asks, "Why do we even need to use a heijunka box if the cycle time is the same as for our confirmed state?"

That is an excellent question and both Jane and Robby explain that a heijunka box will essentially eliminate the need for the cycle counter to check stock because there will be little or no inventory in house for those items not in a supermarket, thus no need to go count them.

The heijunka box will not be implemented until all items that are suitable for a supermarket are set up. Right now that isn't the case. Only a small number of items are in supermarkets, hence why we need to check stock. Moreover, even though the time to check stock is not listed in the confirmed state because it's not part of the buyer process and the buyer no longer has to wait for a count, it still takes time for the cycle counter to go out and count. This event was focused on the buyer, but the heijunka box process will help eliminate steps and transactions for other areas as well.

For non-supermarket purchases: the total time is 33.5 minutes (2007 seconds) compared to Steve's original current state of 160 minutes (9581 seconds), thus a 79% improvement.

Review of current vs. ideal state supermarket process

For the supermarket process, the current state, its corresponding ideal state and the confirmed state are illustrated in Figures 51 - 52 :

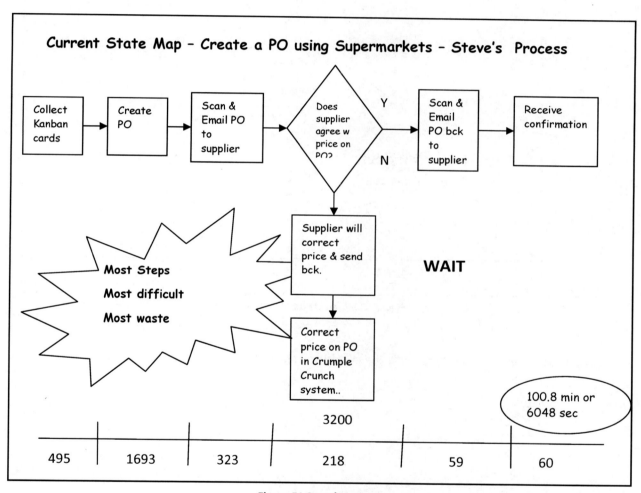

Figure 51 Steve's process.

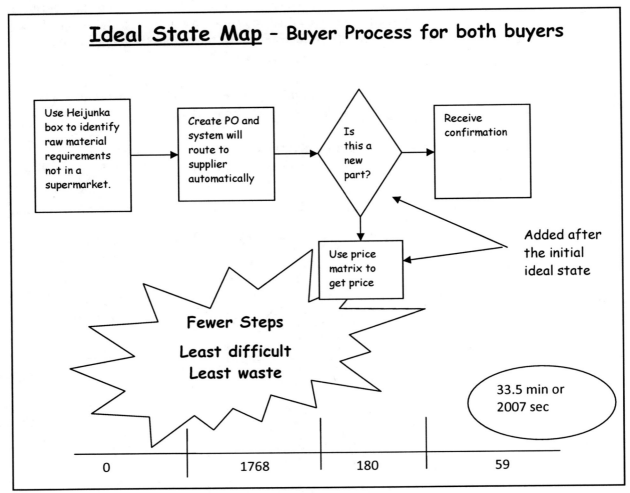

Figure 52 Supermarket Ideal State

The team was able to combine these into the confirmed state shown in Figure 53.

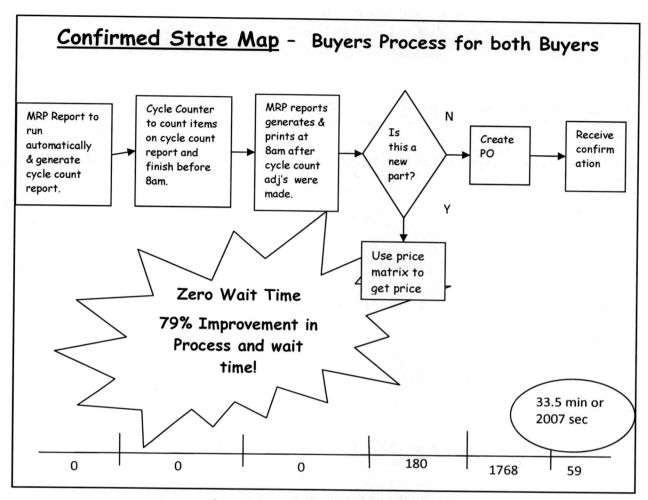

Figure 53 Supermarket Items Confirmed State.

So what led the team to the confirmed state?

The team reviewed all their accomplishments for the week. Here's a recap of their discussion.

As you recall, the ideal state for the supermarket process will not work until the bar code process is in place. Our completion plan states that we will set up a meeting to discuss the next steps for adding bar codes to the kanban cards. Since we're not sure the bar coding will actually be in place within 90 days, we cannot assume we've met our ideal state. We will, however, have the new PO process in place allowing us to scan and e-mail the kanban cards to the supplier in lieu of creating a purchase order every time.

So how do we know if the confirmed state is more efficient than the current state?

Let's add the cycle times to the bottom based on the following information:

Collecting the kanban cards cycle time is 495 seconds, same as in the current state.

Scanning and e-mailing the kanban cards is assumed to be the same cycle time as scanning and e-mailing purchase orders as in the current state of 323 seconds.

Receiving the confirmation is also the same as the current state cycle time of 60 seconds.

> **For supermarket items: the total time is 14.6 minutes (878 seconds) compared to Steve's original current state of 100.8 minutes (6048 seconds), thus an 85.5% improvement.**

Wow! The team was really excited and couldn't wait to present their accomplishments to management!

A3 review

Jane announces, "We're just about done." But there's more to do.

Before completing the event, it's important to go back and review the A3 objectives. The original objectives for this event are listed below:

- Reduce the time to create a purchase order by reducing transactions
- Remove waste and non value added work
- Write Standard Work for new process

Jane asks the team if the objectives were accomplished.

It's pretty clear the answer is definitely "YES." Everyone on the team was happy and proud of their work.

Jane leads the team as they finish out the rest of the boxes on the A3. Their completed A3 is shown in Figure 54.

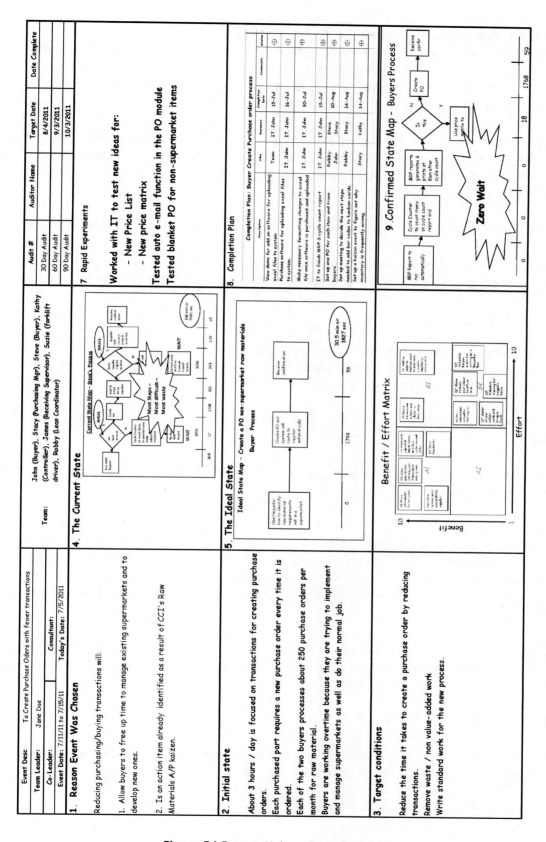

Figure 54 Buyers Kaizen Completed A3

Prepare the team's report

At this point the team was nearing the end of day four, and ready to prepare for their presentation and completion plan. At Crumple Crunch, the team is required to have a Friday morning presentation. Since Jane is familiar with the process, she had already uploaded several of the rapid experiment pictures, the A3, and any other relative information she thought the team would like to share with the audience.

Remember, you are telling a story from beginning to end. It's not all about the results, but how you arrived at the final results. Jane has developed a skill for keeping the audience's attention and ensuring management support when structuring the presentation! She is very clear as to where CCI is today versus where they will be in our confirmed and ideal state.

Jane went over the presentation with the team. The team made some changes and finished the report.

Each team member will present a portion of the presentation so the slides were divided up between them and they decided to practice tomorrow morning, just before the presentation.

Day 5

Report to management

The team presented the final presentation to management and gained full support of their efforts. Steve Stark, CCI's CEO was impressed.

Steve is a strong lean leader; he was especially happy to see rigorous application of lean methods in the back office.

Everyone went away from the meeting feeling energized to execute the Completion Plan and to make sure their good work would "stick."

Follow-ups

Ok, so you've observed two detailed examples of kaizen events in the office. But it's important to remember that even though the team is finished with the kaizen event, they still have many follow-ups on the completion plan. They went away determined not to let the completion plan fall off the radar screen. Likewise, the team leader will do what's possible to sustain the kaizen's accomplishments. Here are some things they can do.

Have weekly follow-up meetings with all team members. Remember, this is not the lean Olympics! You don't have a final presentation – everyone claps and on Monday we go back to doing the same thing we did before the event.

Be vigilant and finish the completion plan.

Not only do we need to finish the completion plan but we have to SUSTAIN THE RESULTS! From experience, this is the main area where companies fail. Don't be one of those companies.

How do we know our improvements are working?

Red dot board

One sure way to know if your improvements are working is to implement a "red dot" board.

In this example, if after the completion plan is finished and the buyers are still having issues in certain areas, Jane would show them how to keep a red dot board.

There are several types of issues that may arise that prevent the buyers from following their Standard Work. The team came up with a few ideas and wrote them on the red dot board. They left some blank lines so that unforeseen issues that come up later can be added. It's not necessary to think of all the types of issues at this time. It's easier to write in a new type of issue once it arises.

The red dot board should be kept in plain view of anyone walking past the buyers' desks. Management can walk by and easily see what types of issues are frequently occurring. It's typical that when new Standard Work is implemented that some overlooked items or mistakes will come to light.

If the manager can get to the root cause of the issues immediately, the odds are better for sustainment.

Once people get used to doing something wrong, or do not even know they are doing something wrong, they are more likely to continue if they are not informed otherwise.

Figure 55 shows the red dot board that CCI's kaizen team created.

CCI BuyersRed Dot - Issues

# of invoices processed / Weeks	Monday	Tuesday	Wednesday	Thursday	Friday	Total
New part size not on matrix						
Cycle counts incorrect						
kanban cards missing						
price wrong on price list						

Figure 55 CCI Buyers Red Dot Board

Note: Too many red dots generally indicates the process is difficult or that someone doesn't know that what they are doing is causing another department an issue.

Another tip: You can also use a red dot board for several weeks BEFORE the event to document the frequency and types of issues occurring. This will help when documenting the current state map. The team will have solid proof of the types of waste and frequency of occurrences in the process.

Going forward

Congratulations!

We are finished with the buyers' kaizen event and it's up to us to make sure we complete the completion plan and also sustain our results through following the Standard Work and keeping a red dot board for those times issues arise.

You now have two kaizens under your belt and should be well on your way to making many improvements along your lean journey.

Finally, CCI's team and Jane spent some time reflecting on the kaizen they just completed.

Because they were new to the kaizen process, they needed time to think about what they had done and the process they used.

In this case, they discussed the brainstorming techniques they used, how well they worked and how the makeup of the team had contributed to the team's success.

This process of reflection – "unpacking" the experience as a group if you will – is a very important piece of learning. With more experience, this reflection will move to discussing some of the deeper issues and the thinking processes the team went though.

Still later and with more experience the team will get busy documenting their learning and leveraging cross-functional learning to the best advantage for the company.

These are essential steps in creating a sustainable lean culture.

What's ahead in the "Cook up Some Change" series and what's next for YOU?

Now's a good time to go back and review the lean office and accounting Diagnostic.

Up to now, CCI's office teams have concentrated their lean efforts on the "Accounts Payable and Procurement" section of the Diagnostic; this is where they've made their improvements.

Are they all done?

No, of course not.

But using the Diagnostic, CCI has effectively moved from "traditional" to "developing a framework" in the "accounts payable and procurement" area.

CCI will do more events in the other areas of the Diagnostic. They will continue to use the Diagnostic as way to chart their course and assess their progress.

It appears the next logical step will be to finish the buyers' completion plan, by scheduling an event to see why inventory is frequently wrong.

Oh, and Jane has witnessed A/P actually using the new auto-match process. The A/P clerk and the controller are also talking about pay on receipt. How cool is that?

In the beginning stages of lean, kaizen events bring about the greatest improvements.

As companies move more toward "lean business management" and as lean culture and methods take root and flourish, it's often the case they will make some improvements without actually doing an "event."

Sometimes it's that first event that sets the stage for the "ideal state." Once the ideal state has been envisioned and set in place, employees sometimes begin making improvements to target the ideal state without events. We call these improvements "just do its." In other words, after a number of events, "change" becomes a way of life. As you get further into the lean process, don't think it's a "must" to have a full blown event to make an improvement.

This volume is only the beginning.

Stay tuned to see how CCI continues on their lean journey using the Diagnostic to track their progress.

BMA Press will be publishing additional guides that can help you get change going in your office, sustain it, and move your entire operation to Lean Business Management.

CPSIA information can be obtained at www.ICGtesting.com
Printed in the USA
LVOW031941050912

297563LV00004B/1/P